TERRORIST FINANCING

Finance Matters

Series Editors: Kathryn Lavelle, Case Western Reserve University, Cleveland, Ohio and Timothy J. Sinclair, University of Warwick

This series of books provides advanced introductions to the processes, relationships and institutions that make up the global financial system. Suitable for upper-level undergraduate and taught graduate courses in financial economics and the political economy of finance and banking, the series explores all aspects of the workings of the financial markets within the context of the broader global economy.

Published

Banking on the State: The Political Economy of Public Savings Banks
Mark K. Cassell

British Business Banking: The Failure of Finance Provision for SMEs
Michael Lloyd

Credit Rating Agencies
Giulia Mennillo

The European Central Bank
Michael Heine and Hansjörg Herr

Quantitative Easing: The Great Central Bank Experiment
Jonathan Ashworth

Regulating Banks: The Politics of Instability
Andrew Whitworth

Sovereign Wealth Funds: Between the State and Markets
Adam D. Dixon, Patrick J. Schena and Javier Capapé

Terrorist Financing
William Vlcek

TERRORIST FINANCING

WILLIAM VLCEK

First published in 2022 by Agenda Publishing

Agenda Publishing Limited
The Core
Bath Lane
Newcastle Helix
Newcastle upon Tyne
NE4 5TF
www.agendapub.com

ISBN 978-1-78821-527-5 (hardcover)
ISBN 978-1-78821-528-2 (paperback)

British Library Cataloguing-in-Publication Data
A catalogue record for this book is available from the British Library

Typeset by Newgen Publishing UK
Printed and bound in the UK by TJ Books

CONTENTS

PREFACE AND ACKNOWLEDGEMENTS

The aim of this book is to provide an overview of terrorist finance in the twenty-first century and the measures employed to identify and obstruct money intended to support acts of terrorism. Terrorist financing has been a concern and topic of analysis for a large number of policy-makers and academics throughout the past two decades (and longer for a few specialists). In large part, the attention has been focused on the group or groups that represented a threat to a specific country. When the terrorist threat is local, and thus a national problem, this concern is understandable. Yet the dynamic changed at the end of the twentieth century with the emergence of a more transnational form of terrorism. In turn, the states affected by transnational terrorist groups turned their efforts towards an international campaign against terrorist financing as one modality for suppressing and preventing acts of terrorism. The initial result was the construction of mechanisms to combat the financing of terrorism (CFT) suitable for operation in the financial systems of developed economies. In time the international guidance evolved to offer some flexibility for implementation that recognized the different circumstances operating in the financial systems of a developing economy. A similar distinction can be found in the literature on terrorist finance, where a large part remains concerned with the financial systems of developed economies and a small portion analyses the impact of CFT measures on economic development, financial inclusion and the limited reach of formal finance in the developing economies.

The following chapters are the product of close to 20 years studying global finance and seeking to understand the efforts taken by national and international authorities to regulate and govern it. Much of the focus for this activity is located at the intersection of finance and security, and terrorist finance has been one of the central concerns. This text builds on research published in a number of edited books and academic journals, and it follows the general structure developed for a fourth-year undergraduate module at the University of St Andrews that I taught between 2009 and 2012. To access the publications and guidelines of the Financial Action Task Force and United Nations Security Council, mentioned throughout the text, please see the References section, which provides the general web addresses for these organizations through which the various publications can then be found.

I want to thank Agenda Publishing and Alison Howson for this opportunity to share my perspective on the subject. Over the past two decades a number of colleagues have commented on my work and my thanks to all of them: Javier Argomaniz, Faye Donnelly, Rikard Jalkebro, Yee Kuang Heng, Rashmi Singh, Jorge Lasmar, Yannick Veilleux-Lepage, Christopher J. Hill, Karen E. Smith, Andrew Neal, Didier Bigo, Anthony Amicelle, Oldrich Bures, Christian Kaunert, Sarah Léonard, Raphael Bossong, Anja Jakobi, Mark Nance, Nikos Passas and Jason Sharman. Because this covers a long time period, I apologize to anyone that I may have missed. Faye Donnelly has been especially generous with her time, reading the entire manuscript and providing detailed feedback on it. All the same, any error that may be present here is solely my responsibility.

ACRONYMS AND ABBREVIATIONS

AML	Anti-money laundering
ACH	Automated Clearing House
BMPE	Black Market Peso Exchange
CDD	Customer due diligence
CFT	Combatting/Countering the financing of terrorism
CIA	Central Intelligence Agency
CoE	Council of Europe
CTC	Counter-Terrorism Committee
CTED	Counterterrorism Committee Executive Directorate
CVV	Card verification value
DNFBPs	Designated non-financial businesses and professions
ESAAMLG	Eastern and Southern Africa Anti-Money Laundering Group
ELN	Ejército de Liberación Nacional
EU	European Union
FARC	Fuerzas Armadas Revolucionarias de Colombia
FATF	Financial Action Task Force
FBI	Federal Bureau of Investigation
FinCEN	Financial Crimes Enforcement Network
FIU	Financial intelligence units
FSRB	FATF-style regional body
GDP	Gross domestic product
GDPR	General Data Protection Regulation
GSMA	Groupe Spéciale Mobile Association
ILO	International Labour Organization
IMF	International Monetary Fund
INLA	Irish National Liberation Army
IRA	Irish Republican Army
IS	Islamic State
ISIL	Islamic State in Iraq and the Levant

ISIS	Islamic State of Iraq and Syria
IVTS	Informal value transfer service
KYC	Know your customer
LTTE	Liberation Tigers of Tamil Eelam
MMO	Mobile money operator
MSB	Money service business
NCCT	Non-cooperative countries and territories
NGO	Non-governmental organization
NORAID	Irish Northern Aid Committee
NPO	Non-profit organization
POS	Point of sale
RBA	Risk-based approach
RUSI	Royal United Services Institute
SAR	Suspicious activity report
STR	Suspicious transaction report
SDG	Sustainable Development Goal
SEPA	Single Euro Payments Area
TFTP	Terrorist Finance Tracking Programme
UN	United Nations
USA PATRIOT Act	Uniting and Strengthening America by Providing Appropriate Tools Required to Intercept and Obstruct Terrorism (USA PATRIOT) Act of 2001

1

FOUNDATIONS AND ORIGINS

The United Nations (UN) opened the treaty entitled "International Convention for the Suppression of the Financing of Terrorism" for signature in 1999.[1] Over a year later, on 10 September 2001, a grand total of four states had signed and ratified the treaty: Botswana, Sri Lanka, the United Kingdom and Uzbekistan. The events of 11 September 2001 and the response, individually and collectively, to the terrorist attacks on New York City and Washington, DC changed the need and utility for this particular UN Convention. Financial surveillance and the tracking of the economic activity of individuals and groups would be massively increased as a leading element of the new "war on terror". Measures to combat the financing of terrorism (CFT) would be crafted and all countries would be expected to introduce them to their national legal systems.[2]

This book seeks to provide you with an understanding of why there were so few ratifications of the UN Convention on terrorist financing in September 2001 as compared to September 2002. The Convention entered into force on 10 April 2002 following the 22nd ratification of it. Further, you will gain an understanding of the development and evolution of the global regime to combat terrorist financing in the first two decades of the twenty-first century. This chapter prepares you with several background concepts to establish a foundation for the material covered in the remaining chapters. The next section begins with a definition of terrorism as a political act, a necessary prerequisite for defining terrorist finance. But first there is a section developing the concept of money that is implied in the activity of terrorist financing. Following the definition of terrorist financing, drawn from the UN Convention, the chapter offers some background on the Financial Action Task Force (FATF), the international organization created to address money laundering by illegal drugs traffickers. It would be drafted into international efforts against terrorism in 2001, and attempt to apply its existing expertise developed to counter money laundering to terrorist financing. The final section of this chapter points towards the topics covered in each of the remaining chapters of the book.

Definitions

A constant element present in many discussions of terrorism includes the debate on its definition (English 2016: 136–7). This book is no different in placing the issue of definition in the first chapter. A central point of disagreement in the definition is over who is in and who is out, which group is named as being a "terrorist" group and which group is not named as such. Part of the reason for the definitional debate involves the politics of naming (Bhatia 2008). For a government to identify a group or organization as terrorist is a political act as much as it is a legal one to authorize the use of anti-terrorist legislation against the group. The political element places the emotion-laden connotations associated with "terrorist" on the group and all of its actions and activities. When those activities are acknowledged and receive support from other countries and groups, because they are seen as anti-colonial or anti-authoritarian, there is pushback and resistance to the act of naming. This distinction is revisited in Chapter 5 because resistance to the act of naming was a factor in some countries in opposing the introduction of CFT legislation. National experience with political violence shapes a country's engagement with the international regime against terrorism.

The basic definitional proposition that one person's *terrorist* is another person's *freedom fighter* is simplistic. It seeks to justify the actions of those groups that a speaker supports – that is the freedom fighter acting on behalf of the oppressed people – while at the same time condemning the individuals or groups that the same speaker opposes – the terrorists who are killing innocent bystanders for illegitimate reasons. Fundamentally, terrorism is *political violence*; it is a violent act intended to create fear in a target audience for political purposes. For this book, terrorism is understood as a label that identifies the actions of a non-state actor, in either a domestic or an international context. Whether you will agree with the designation of someone as a terrorist will depend on your point of view, and your position on the issue that is used to justify the use of violence. This situation is reflected in the failure to reach an international agreement on a definition for terrorism. In part this is due to the use of the term terrorist as a pejorative label or an insult. By labelling our political opponents as terrorists we make them appear as less legitimate, in turn reducing the legitimacy of their political claims. Essentially, we must accept that it is not just terrorism that is a political act but also our use of the word as a label.

The proposition that state actors and their representatives also engage in acts of terrorism is left aside in this book. The international regime to combat the financing of terrorism only covers the actions of non-state actors. For the case of state terrorism, states have their own resources to draw on for financing their use of violence. Separate from the designation of state terrorism, there is the case of states supporting the activities of a terrorist group. State sponsors of terrorism are addressed through other measures, including economic sanctions. Countries named as "state sponsors of terrorism" are present in Chapter 2 as part of the discussion on terrorist financing in the twentieth century.[3]

For the purposes of this book terrorism consists of political violence performed by non-state actors. This is a simplification of the more comprehensive definition offered by Richard English in *Terrorism: How to Respond*:

> Terrorism involves heterogeneous violence used or threatened with a political aim; it can involve a variety of acts, of targets, and of actors; it possesses an important psychological dimension, producing terror or fear among a directly threatened group and also a wider implied audience in the hope of maximizing political communication and achievement; it embodies the exerting and implementing of power, and the attempted redressing of power-relations; it represents a subspecies of warfare, and as such it can form part of a wider campaign of violent and nonviolent attempts at political leverage.   (English 2009: 24)

With this definition we must accept the fact that it is the state that names and identifies the terrorist. And that it is the state that seeks to suppress and interdict the activities of those it has designated as terrorists. State actors, and their representatives in international organizations, have created this international regime against terrorism and its financing.

What is money?

Before moving onto the definition of terrorist financing, let us briefly turn our attention to money. It is true that terrorism may be financed by a variety of assets, including the sale of used cars, trafficking in illegal drugs and credit card fraud. Ultimately, however, those involved hope to convert the asset into money because it is more fungible. That is, money, commonly in the form of cash, is easily exchanged for the goods and services needed by the terrorist group. Importantly, cash is also anonymous, with no clear connection back to the person that used it. As demonstrated in the following chapters, terrorist groups finance themselves any number of ways, but money as currency notes and coins is the easiest form to use in pursuit of their political goals.

For economists, money performs three main functions, and these remain the same regardless of whether we use printed currency, minted coins, gold bullion, sea shells, glass beads or some other easily exchanged portable tokens. Money serves as a medium of exchange; a store of value; and a unit of account (Ingham 2004; Dodd 2014). As a medium of exchange, money represents a value that is then used as payment for goods, services or other property. So you can take a currency note from your wallet and use it to pay for a coffee at your local café. In doing so, the inefficiencies of bartering are removed from the transaction. The currency note provides the means for converting your labour into a form that allows you to acquire the product of other people's labour, including the farmer that grew and harvested the coffee beans, the roaster that prepared the beans and sold them to the café, and the barista that carefully ground, prepared and poured your favourite cup of coffee.

You are able to accomplish the vital task of paying for your cup of coffee because the note is also a store of value. That means it represents a specific amount that is exchangeable for any variety of things that are deemed to have a similar or lesser value. As a store of value, you may carry the note around in your wallet for an indeterminate amount of time before exchanging it for a good or a service. You could also put it in a jar at home and save it with other notes for some future exchange that will require a larger value than what the individual note represents. Alternatively, you could store it at the bank, where it is translated into a notation representing the fact that the bank has added that amount of exchange value to your account. This means that your debit card is a medium of exchange but it is not a store of value because it represents some unknown value in your account at the bank. As long as there is sufficient value to cover your purchase, that is all that is necessary to complete the transaction using a debit card.

Finally, a currency note is also a unit of account. The note is denominated with a designated value that represents, indirectly, the value placed on your labour as well as the value placed on the labour of everyone involved in creating and providing the good or service that is received in exchange for it. This labour value is in addition to the value placed on the commodities used to create the product, such as the raw coffee beans. One point to understand and appreciate here is that nowhere in this economic discussion is an ethical or moral status assigned to the money. It is our intentionality in how we wish to exchange the product of our labour to support a cause that possesses an ethical or moral dimension. It is, in other words, the individual's sense of ethics and morality that motivates the decision to contribute to an environmental or religious charity. Equally, the person's belief in the goals of the terrorist group will lead them to contribute, financially and materially, to help the group to achieve its goals.

This factor highlights the point that while money is rather fundamental to all economic transactions, we do not really think about it in any conscious manner. It brings into the discussion the sociology of money, because money, in the form of currency notes or coins from your wallet, or the electronic data attached to your bank account and represented by a debit card, is a *constructed* concept. That is, we as a society have constructed this concept of money, we mutually agree to it and we operate as an economic organization or as a market as if money is a physical fact in the same way that we treat a table as a physical fact.

It is also important to appreciate that, within the operation of these economic transactions, money plays a critical and crucial role as a social relation, as well as being the product of social relations (Ingham 1996). Where money performs the function of a medium of exchange it provides a lubricant for social relations, facilitating the exchange of goods and services among disparate actors. It is the means to transform my labour so that I may benefit (and perhaps profit) from your labour. Thus, for a network of social relations, money is a flow in the network moving in opposition to the flow (exchange) of a good and/or service. In this understanding, money is not simply a mechanism by which to transform one's labour into a medium of exchange for the results of the labour of other people. Beyond the economic functions performed by money, social meaning is assigned or given to it by the individual. Social meaning exists in the notion of setting currency notes aside in a jar for some future transaction. The jar holds the purpose of that transaction, for purchasing holiday gifts, for spending during a vacation, or for a new washing machine, settee or car. This practice is known as "earmarking", assigning a purpose with symbolic meaning to the money that reflects its intended future purpose (Zelizer 1989).

Consequently, it is important to recognize that it is much the same with terrorist financing; it is money that has been set aside to contribute to the group. And it is in support of its goals that individuals willingly and knowingly contribute to the group. They are providing money in conscious support and encouragement of the violence that will be used in pursuit of those political goals. In other words, they have "earmarked" this money to donate for use by the group, to include its use for the planning and execution of an act of terrorism. In turn, it is this logic that lies behind legally defining the practice of terrorist financing as a criminal act. Yet the complexities involved in establishing laws that criminalize terrorist finance without interfering with the financing of non-violent politics is reflected in the intricate definition produced for terrorist financing in the UN treaty, as explored in the next section.

An international definition of terrorist financing

The definition developed in the International Convention for the Suppression of the Financing of Terrorism at Article 2 is structured in a legal form. The presentation immediately lends itself to transposition into national legislation and criminal code as directed by Article 4 of the treaty.

Article 2:

1. Any person commits an offence within the meaning of this Convention if that person by any means, directly or indirectly, unlawfully and wilfully, provides or collects funds with the intention that they should be used or in the knowledge that they are to be used, in full or in part, in order to carry out:

    (a) An act which constitutes an offence within the scope of and as defined in one of the treaties listed in the annex; or

    (b) Any other act intended to cause death or serious bodily injury to a civilian, or to any other person not taking an active part in the hostilities in a situation of armed conflict, when the purpose of such act, by its nature or context, is to intimidate a population, or to compel a government or an international organization to do or to abstain from doing any act.

2. ...

3. For an act to constitute an offence set forth in paragraph 1, it shall not be necessary that the funds were actually used to carry out an offence referred to in paragraph 1, subparagraphs (a) or (b).

4. Any person also commits an offence if that person attempts to commit an offence as set forth in paragraph 1 of this article.

5. ...

The second paragraph of this Article concerns the relationship between the ratification of this treaty and the state's ratification of the other UN treaties on terrorism (Table 1.1). The remaining paragraphs (4 and 5) of Article 2 specify how to identify a person involved in the financing of terrorism as defined in the treaty. The nine treaties listed in Table 1.1, from the Annex of the Convention, address specific forms of terrorism that were of concern at the time the treaty was drafted, for example the spate of aircraft hijackings in the late 1960s and 1970s. In addition to the specific activities covered by the treaties, paragraph 1(b) incorporates any other act of political violence intended to strike terror in the target audience. It is, in essence, the definition of terrorism for the purposes of the treaty.

There is a further point to observe about the International Convention for the Suppression of the Financing of Terrorism in the contents of Article 3.

This Convention shall not apply where the offence is committed within a single State, the alleged offender is a national of that State and is present in the territory of that State and no other State has a basis under article 7, paragraph 1, or article 7, paragraph 2, to exercise jurisdiction, except that the provisions of articles 12 to 18 shall, as appropriate, apply in those cases.

Table 1.1 International Conventions on terrorism, as of 1999

1. Convention for the Suppression of Unlawful Seizure of Aircraft, The Hague, 16 December 1970.
2. Convention for the Suppression of Unlawful Acts against the Safety of Civil Aviation, Montreal, 23 September 1971.
3. Convention on the Prevention and Punishment of Crimes against Internationally Protected Persons, including Diplomatic Agents, adopted by the General Assembly of the UN, 14 December 1973.
4. International Convention against the Taking of Hostages, adopted by the General Assembly of the UN, 17 December 1979.
5. Convention on the Physical Protection of Nuclear Material, Vienna, 3 March 1980.
6. Protocol for the Suppression of Unlawful Acts of Violence at Airports Serving International Civil Aviation, supplementary to the Convention for the Suppression of Unlawful Acts against the Safety of Civil Aviation, Montreal, 24 February 1988.
7. Convention for the Suppression of Unlawful Acts against the Safety of Maritime Navigation, Rome, 10 March 1988.
8. Protocol for the Suppression of Unlawful Acts against the Safety of Fixed Platforms located on the Continental Shelf, Rome, 10 March 1988.
9. International Convention for the Suppression of Terrorist Bombings, adopted by the General Assembly of the UN, 15 December 1997.

Source: Annex, International Convention for the Suppression of the Financing of Terrorism (1999).

As written, this Article restricts terrorist financing to groups and activities with an international component. If the funds, fund raiser and intended recipient all reside within the territorial boundaries of a single state, the provisions of the treaty will not apply. We may expect that any country that has transposed the treaty into domestic law has also made it applicable to wholly domestic terrorism. At the same time, it may be difficult to identify a terrorist group that does not have some cross-border connection, which could be the location of a fugitive member or the source of weapons and other material support in addition to financial support.

There are two operational dimensions contained in the definition of terrorist financing. First, there is the process of collecting the money needed to support the individual and group, both for day-to-day operations of the group and for conducting a specific act of terrorism. This dimension is clearly reflected in paragraph 1 of Article 2, and fundraising is targeted by CFT measures. Measures to combat terrorist financing, however, may have limited success in recognizing a case where the terrorist group is self-funded (Keatinge & Keen 2017b). The second dimension involves the process of transferring that money to the terrorist group. This aspect is far more present in CFT practices, relying as it does on the same methods and techniques used for identifying and interdicting money laundering. This feature of the international regime against terrorist finance is introduced in the following section, which presents the FATF, which will be revisited throughout the following chapters. There is a tension created by the use of anti-money laundering (AML) methods to combat terrorist financing. Where AML is pursuing the proceeds of crime (illegal money), it is not the case that all money used to finance terrorism comes from a criminal source. In fact, money to support a terrorist group could be from something as simple as an individual depositing a portion of their wages into a collection cup at the local shop.

The situation results in a legal money/illegal money dichotomy. In turn, the application of AML laws to terrorist finance may be problematic, depending on the legal system. The remedy for addressing terrorist finance when it involves legal money is to move away from focusing on the source of the money and instead turn to the fact that the money is *intended* to be used to finance terrorism. The intentionality dimension is captured in the phrase "intended to be used or with the knowledge that it will be used" for acts of terrorism in the definition of the UN treaty. It also means that in order to charge someone with the crime of terrorist financing, the prosecutor needs to demonstrate that the accused knew the contribution was to support terrorism, or that the accused intended for the contribution to be used to support terrorism. Presenting the necessary evidence in open court without using information the government wants kept secret may be one factor limiting the number of prosecutions for terrorist financing. For example, Leuprecht *et al.* (2019) collected data on 32 civil and criminal court cases for their analysis. They described this set of cases as "the universe of known transnational terrorist resourcing cases for which sufficient open-source data exists" (292).

The effort made to disguise the source and origins of money used to finance terrorism has been named "reverse money laundering" by some commentators (e.g. Cassella 2002: 11). Where money laundering is the process to conceal the criminal origins of the proceeds of crime, using the description of "reverse money laundering" exposes a purpose to protect the identity of those supporting the terrorist group. Using a laundering process helps to conceal the source of financing and to protect contributors from being charged with terrorist finance. Where the cash donations to a collection cup will be anonymous, the shop owner hosting the cup could be charged with terrorist financing because they know of the intended purpose of the money collected.

Foundations of the international regime: the FATF

The concern with illegal money and identifying methods for dealing with it emerged in the 1980s. The central issue of concern was illegal drugs trafficking and the substantial sums of money generated by the sale of them. One strategy was to focus on "money laundering", as the process used by criminals to conceal the illegal origins of their income (Nance 2018: 113–14). The Financial Action Task Force (FATF) was initially created in 1989 to determine how money laundering worked, what measures were already being taken against it, and then to produce international standards to guide national efforts against money laundering. In addition to preventing money laundering, there was a desire to "follow the money" as a mechanism to identify and convict the traffickers (Wechsler 2001). The logic is that if law enforcement finds it difficult to charge the leader of a drugs trafficking gang with illegal drugs-related crimes, the alternative is to charge them with possession of the criminal profits of illegal drugs trafficking.[4] In the case of the US, the representative example justifying this law enforcement strategy is Al Capone. Widely known as an organized crime gang leader involved in bootlegging during Prohibition, he was never convicted for any of his alleged crimes. Instead, Capone was convicted of tax evasion, for failing to pay income tax on his illegal income (van Duyne, Harvey & Gelemerova 2018: 41–2). Alongside this tale is the story that he sought to conceal the criminal origins of his money by owning pool halls and laundromats, claiming that they were the source for all of his income (Sharman 2011: 16).

The first report from the FATF included its Recommendations for AML guidance and legislation. These Recommendations numbered 40, and ever since have been known as the "Forty Recommendations". The initial focus of the FATF and their AML recommendations was drugs trafficking. The first Recommendation stated that all states should ratify the UN Convention Against Illicit Traffic in Narcotic Drugs and Psychotropic Substances, 1988, also known as the Vienna Convention.[5] The term "money laundering" is not present in this UN Convention, rather it refers to the "proceeds of crime". The focus with the first set of FATF Recommendations was to support the implementation of the Vienna Convention and the international campaign against illegal drugs trafficking. As initially written, however, the Recommendations were not always understood by the agencies attempting to implement them. The FATF rectified this by creating a set of Interpretative Notes to clarify and explain the intention behind the Recommendations.

The initial version of the Forty Recommendations was revised in 1996 to incorporate the experience from the first years of implementation. It included revised interpretive notes to reflect an expanded understanding of the nature of money laundering and it extended the coverage of AML obligations beyond the initial set of banks and non-bank financial institutions. The revision expanded the scope to include any firm involved in activities such as money transmitting, money lending and life insurance. In October 2001 the FATF held an extraordinary meeting in Washington, DC at which it introduced eight Special Recommendations on Terrorist Financing. These changes are discussed further in Chapter 3. An additional revision to the Forty Recommendations in 2003 brought even more firms within the reporting scope of AML. These "designated non-financial businesses and professions" (DNFBPs) included casinos, lawyers and real estate agents, in an effort to address the shift of money laundering activity away from the banking sector.

To say that money laundering is the process of making illegal income appear as if it is legal income does not explain how the process operates. Money laundering is commonly explained as consisting of three steps: placement, layering and integration.[6] The placement step consists of putting the illegal money into the financial system. Laundromats, pool halls and any other cash-intensive business can serve this purpose. With a cash-intensive business it involves mixing the cash from the criminal activity in with the cash generated by the business and depositing it all at the bank as income from the business. Naturally there are many other ways to get one's illegal money placed, including through the use of cooperative and complicit bank employees (Truell 1996). Simply placing the money into a bank account is likely not enough to conceal its criminal origins if there is a police investigation. The layering step serves to make the success of any investigation difficult, with impossible to succeed being the desired goal. In this phase the money is moved through a series of transactions, which may involve the purchase and sale of goods in addition to transfers between multiple financial institutions. The introduction of AML reporting obligations for non-financial businesses is intended to expose possible layering of illegal money. When the layering phase is considered complete, the final step, integration of the money, has been achieved. With integration the money has found its way back to the beneficial owner, appearing now as if it comes from a completely legitimate source.[7]

The techniques used for the placement and layering steps are many and varied. Much of what is known about the actual practice of money laundering comes from those that have been caught. Additionally, government and law enforcement officials seek to identify other potential forms of economic activity that could be used to launder illegal money. The FATF collates and disseminates this information through Methods and Trends or Typology reports.[8] They often contain anonymized case studies describing examples of money laundering where the participants were caught and convicted. The reports often focus on a specific form of economic activity, including casinos, free trade zones and *hawala*, a traditional money transfer system that is discussed in Chapters 3 and 5.

Another feature of the FATF that appears to influence the nature of the AML/CFT guidance produced is the membership of the organization. Beginning as a small, select group of states, the FATF is an example of a "club" intergovernmental organization (Hülsse 2008; Tsingou 2015). The initial membership in 1989 is shown in Table 1.2: the G7 states that called for study of existing

Table 1.2 Original membership of the FATF

Australia	Japan*
Austria	Luxembourg
Belgium	Netherlands
Canada*	Spain
European Commission*	Sweden
France*	Switzerland
Germany*	United Kingdom*
Italy*	United States*

*G7 member.
Source: *FATF on Money Laundering Report* (1990) (accessed 21 March 2002).

Table 1.3 Current membership of the FATF (2021)

Argentina (2000)	France	Japan	Saudi Arabia (2019)
Australia	Germany	Republic of Korea (2009)	Singapore (1992)
Austria	Greece (1991)	Luxembourg	South Africa (2003)
Belgium	Gulf Co-operation Council (n.d.)	Malaysia (2016)	Spain
Brazil (2000)	Hong Kong SAR (1991)	Mexico (2000)	Sweden
Canada	Iceland (1992)	Netherlands, Kingdom of*	Switzerland
China (2007)	India (2010)	New Zealand (1991)	Turkey (1991)
Denmark (1991)	Ireland (1991)	Norway (1991)	United Kingdom
European Commission	Israel (2018)	Portugal (1991)	United States
Finland (1991)	Italy	Russian Federation (2003)	

*Comprising the Netherlands, Aruba, Curaçao and Saint Maarten.
Source: https://www.fatf-gafi.org/about/membersandobservers/.

money laundering methods along with the further eight states invited to contribute. The current membership (2021) is listed in Table 1.3, along with each member states' date of entry, and the FATF remains a small, if arguably representative, inter-governmental group. In addition to these member states there are observers from other international organizations and representatives from the private sector that attend the meetings, expanding the scope of input (Nance 2018: 115). Beyond the immediate membership of the FATF, the organization also supports a group of regionally oriented FATF-style regional bodies (FSRBs), formally listed as associate members of the FATF.[9] These groups will include an FATF member state, and they develop regional expertise as well as providing peer support (or peer pressure) for the global AML/CFT government regime (de Oliveira 2018).

The book's structure

Efforts to combat terrorist financing are deeply entangled with the measures introduced to stop money laundering. Advocates for anti-money laundering have, since 2001, often emphasized its role in combatting terrorist financing as a way to promote their moral crusade against criminal money. Often forgotten (or elided) by these advocates is the fact that it is the state that defines criminality and thus what money is to be deemed criminal and what money is legal and legitimate. The law is socially constructed, which means that decriminalization of a specific conduct or a good, in turn, makes the proceeds from providing that good or service legal, erasing the need for money laundering by the provider. Such is the case with money generated by the marijuana business in those US states where recreational use is now legal (Sun 2020). And the story about Al Capone as a bootlegger does not exist without the failed attempt to prohibit alcohol in the US between 1920 and 1933 (Engelmann 1979).

It is not that "crime doesn't pay", rather there is a sense from some commentators that "crime shouldn't pay" (Wechsler 2001). Illegal money is also described as "dirty" money, suggesting that the (perhaps apocryphal) story of the term money laundering originating in the early use of a laundromat to introduce illegal money into a legal bank account is incorrect. Instead, the term may have emerged from the desire to transform "dirty" (illegal) money into "clean" (legal) money. The emotive designation of the proceeds of crime as "dirty" money serves to elicit support from law-abiding citizens so that they accept the intrusion by the government into their individual financial dealings. The AML campaign is accepted because it is the way to deal with the immoral money possessed by criminals. Similar emotive framing is applied to terrorist financing, justifying the surveillance imposed to expose it, as well as acceptance of government actions against anyone accused of financing terrorism without providing evidence for public review and judgement.

The normative dimension of CFT will arise later in the book when considering the impact of the AML/CFT obligation to "know your customer" (KYC) in those countries where a significant portion of the population is unable to provide the necessary formal identification documentation. This obligation serves as a barrier to financial inclusion, and thus it hinders economic development. The remaining chapters are arranged in a chronological and then thematic order. The next chapter provides an examination of terrorist financing and CFT methods during the twentieth century. Chapter 3 then introduces the impact of the 2001 US terrorist attacks on national and international perceptions of the need for CFT. It outlines the immediate response made by the US government along with new Recommendations from the FATF to address terrorist financing. In Chapter 4 the collective effort against terrorist financing through the UN is presented. Beyond the international Convention against terrorist financing the effort includes UN Security Council sanctions against individuals and groups engaged in terrorism, along with others specifically accused of financing terrorism. The efforts of the UN were the first step in a wider campaign to make the CFT regime global. As explained in Chapter 5, this global campaign can be problematic for groups and countries who do not believe they are threatened by transnational terrorism. Money was discussed previously and Chapter 6 covers the topic called "new payment technologies" by the FATF. This term covers a variety of proposed replacements for cash money – bitcoin, other digital currencies, mobile money – which could potentially be used for terrorist financing. The specific case of Islamic State (IS) and terrorist financing is explored in Chapter 7. This case is different from other transnational terrorist groups because it controlled territory for a period of time. The opportunity to exploit other sources of money that comes from controlling territory introduced additional challenges to the CFT regime. The concluding chapter offers several reflections on the efficacy of the CFT regime and its impact on money and finance in the world economy.

2

TERRORIST FINANCING IN THE TWENTIETH CENTURY

The 11 September 2001 attack on the World Trade Center in New York City was not the first attempt to bring the skyscrapers crashing to the ground. On 26 February 1993, Ramzi Yousef drove a Ryder Econoline (rental) van loaded with explosives into the parking garage of the World Trade Center. The detonation of over 1,000 pounds of fertilizer supplemented by hydrogen cylinders left a blast crater of 130 feet by 150 feet with damage to seven levels of the building, killing six people and injuring a further 1,042 people (United States Fire Administration 1993: 1).[1] There is a brief description of attempts to identify and track down those responsible for the attack on the website of the US State Department Diplomatic Security Service. The emphasis of this online article is to highlight the role of the Diplomatic Security Service in the identification and apprehension of Ramzi Yousef, and it contains this interesting statement: "This event was the first indication for the Diplomatic Security Service (DSS) that terrorism was evolving from a regional phenomenon outside of the United States to a transnational phenomenon" (Bureau of Diplomatic Security 2019: n.p.). The statement, to some extent, may be self-reflective, given that the page is dated 21 February 2019. At the same time, however, it reinforces widely held perceptions of terrorism in the twentieth century as fundamentally a local problem.

The case of the first terrorist attack on the World Trade Center is often used to emphasize the importance of money in terrorist groups achieving their objectives (Raphaeli 2003: 60; Biersteker & Eckert 2008: 1). The driver of the van soon made his way to Pakistan, where he was later arrested with the assistance of the Diplomatic Security Service and extradited to the US to stand trial. Meanwhile, soon after the bombing, another member of the group returned to the van rental company hoping to get back the $400 deposit. In testimony before a US Senate subcommittee in 1999, the Director of the Federal Bureau of Investigation (FBI) stated that the attempt made to recover the deposit was because the group had very little funding. It was a mistake that led to the arrest of this terrorist along with other members of the group. Crucially, the lack of funding also meant that they were unable to buy as much of the ingredients for the bomb as they wanted. Director Louis J. Freeh said, "As horrible as that act was, it could very well have been much more devastating" (Committee on Appropriations 1999: 45). Emphasizing this point, Jodi Vittori points out that they only had $400 to buy fertilizer for making the bomb (Vittori 2011: 125).

This case serves to demonstrate the importance of actively combatting the financing of terrorism. At the same time, it exposes the limited scope of the claim made that terrorist groups in the twentieth century relied on the support of state sponsors. This group, and many others, were essentially self-funded, while the attention of government officials at the beginning of the 1990s continued to focus on state sponsors of terrorism. This chapter will explore the claim in more detail as it presents the nature of terrorist financing in the latter half of the century. It begins by considering state-sponsored terrorism in the context of the Cold War narrative, which preceded the focus on terrorist financing as a distinct activity that emerged in the 1990s.

The usual story: state-sponsored terrorism

As explained in Chapter 1 (Table 1.1) the international treaties against terrorism before 1999 addressed specific forms or acts of terrorism.[2] The terrorist groups of the 1960s, 1970s and 1980s were largely national in membership, scope and activities.[3] These groups included Black September, Irish Republican Army (IRA), Red Army Faction (Baader-Meinhof Group) and Red Brigades, which focused respectively on the politics of Palestine, Northern Ireland, West Germany and Italy. The locus of terrorism in the 1970s seemed to be Western Europe, shifting to Latin America in the 1980s where leftist political groups confronted military governments and challenged US political influence. One aspect of contemporary analysis on state-sponsored terrorism was the limited attention given to the source of any terrorist group's funding. It is implied by the concept of "state-sponsored" that financial as well as material support for the group was provided by its sponsoring state. Financial support was, essentially, a "feature of state-sponsored terrorism" (Wilkinson 1984: 294–5).

The political violence of the terrorist group serves to bring attention to its cause and attempts to influence the decision-making of the target government. In turn, sponsoring a terrorist group may be seen to serve a similar purpose for the sponsoring state, only to influence the foreign policy decision-making of other states. Paul Wilkinson suggested that a state sponsor was simply exporting the violence it used domestically to control its population (Wilkinson 1984: 292). Along the same line of thinking, Walter Laqueur wrote that state-sponsored terrorism was "mainly the instrument of dictators with ambitions far in excess of their power base" (Laqueur 1986: 95). From this perspective, only repressive state regimes would provide support to a terrorist group. It leaves aside the groups supported by democratic governments as part of their foreign policy, such as US support for anti-Soviet groups in Afghanistan under the occupation of the Soviet Union in the 1980s. The latter point underscores the presence of a Cold War dynamic in considerations of state-sponsored terrorism; in particular, with support given to groups seeking to overthrow an incumbent government where that government would respond by naming the group as "terrorists". This strategy is a phenomenon that continues to the present day.

Nonetheless, it was a focus on state-sponsored terrorism that led the US government to identify specific states on a list. This approach was intended to change the behaviour of listed governments so they stopped supporting terrorist groups by subjecting them to economic sanctions. The list is maintained by the Department of State and currently includes Cuba, North Korea, Iran and Syria.[4] In the past, it has also included Iraq, Libya, South Yemen and Sudan. An annual report provides an explanation for a state's inclusion, with reference to contemporary events and the activities it was accused of supporting. The annual State Department report in 1990, for example, listed various groups in Asia and Latin America that have received support from Cuba, Iran, Iraq, Libya, North Korea and Syria.[5] The use of sanctions against the countries listed as state-sponsors of terrorism is intended as a measure "short of war" (Wallensteen & Staibano 2005). The US government has, however, on occasion, found it necessary to take direct action where diplomatic efforts and sanctions have failed. The attack on Libya in 1986 is a prominent example, when a terrorist attack on a Berlin discotheque popular with US military personnel that spring was the latest in a series of terrorist attacks attributed to Libya, leading to an aerial bombardment in April 1986.

For all the attention focused on the support provided by these countries to terrorist and insurgent groups, these state sponsors were not the only source of money. Establishing a diversity of income sources also may be desirable for the group. For example, the sponsor may insist on imposing their objectives on the operation of the group, or may withdraw support when they do not approve of a terrorist attack (Vittori 2011: 85–6; citing Byman 2005: 5–6). In Europe, the Red Army Faction and Red Brigades self-financed through criminal activities, including extortion, illegal drugs trafficking, kidnapping and robbery (Giraldo & Trinkunas 2007a). These alternatives to state sponsorship are explored in the following four sections, looking first at this European experience up to the end of the century. The case of the UK and the financing of the IRA is considered in a little more detail in the second section, followed in the third section by the fundraising work of Fuerzas Armadas Revolucionarias de Colombia (FARC) in Colombia. The fourth section introduces the financing behind al Qaida for its attacks against US targets outside of North America prior to its 2001 terrorist attack.

The European experience

One approach to understanding the organization of leftist terrorist groups in Europe in the 1970s and 1980s would be to visualize it as a pyramid. At the peak of the pyramid were the core members of the group, who were fully involved in direct action against the government and the institutions of the state. Immediately below them was a layer formed by a larger group that provided support to the core members. Finally, the broad base of the pyramid was comprised of those people sympathetic to the cause and indirectly supporting the core members. It is a useful visualization that equally may be applied to any civil society organization, with a core membership, actively engaged supporters and sympathizers that regularly pay their dues but may not participate in more than the occasional group activity. For sympathizers of a terrorist group, however, to pay dues or otherwise contribute materially to the group is to be involved in terrorist financing. And similar to the experience of many civil society organizations, membership dues are not enough to cover the group's operational costs, making additional fundraising activities necessary. Terrorist groups are no different in that respect, and a Rand report in 1984 not only highlighted several specific fundraising activities for the Red Army Faction in West Germany but also explained the nature of its ongoing costs. A bank robbery in 1982 gained $50,000 for the Red Army Faction, but the authors of the report argued that bank robberies should be understood as indicating financial difficulties because of the risk of arrest (Cordes *et al.* 1984: 36–7).

The Rand report further described the operational methods of the Red Army Faction, with its core members evading capture by continually moving among safe houses. When any member was arrested, every safe house that they may have known about became too risky. For example, three members were arrested in November 1982, which required the gang to abandon old safe houses and rent new ones. It was estimated to cost $50,000 a year (in 1982 US dollars) to support a single core member and protect them from the West German security services. At the time it was thought that there were still 20 core members at large, requiring an annual budget of $1,000,000 (Cordes *et al.* 1984: 37). The 1982 bank robbery was only going to cover a small part of that year's operational costs. A more recent study of the Red Army Faction summarized its record across the period of its recognized existence (1970–98), with 31 robberies raising a total of 7,000,000 deutsche marks ($2.88 million at an exchange rate of 2.43 DM/$1 in 1982) and over 1,000 people being convicted of membership in a terrorist group or supporting one (Moghadam 2012: 157–8).

The cross-border activities of these otherwise domestic European terrorist groups, particularly their criminal fundraising, led to an early European effort to address the problem. The Council of Europe (CoE) is an international organization promoting human rights, democracy and the rule of law across the region. As part of this mission, it considers organized crime and terrorism as a threat to the rule of law.[6] The "Background information" published on the CoE website in 2008 asserted that it "was the first international organisation which emphasised the importance of taking measures to be used for combating the dangers of money laundering" (on file with the author). It would go on to produce several Recommendations and Conventions on money laundering, confiscation of the proceeds of crime and terrorist financing.[7] Work on the first Recommendation began in 1977 and was published in 1980. The steps identified in "Measures Against the Transfer and Safekeeping of Funds of Criminal Origin" (Rec(80)10E) are familiar to us today for the identification and prevention of money laundering (Gilmore 2011: 174–5). The specific recommendations addressed to the member governments were to verify customer identity, improve international cooperation and record the serial numbers of currency notes known to be connected to a criminal act. The Recommendation suggested that a system should be created allowing banks to verify deposited currency against the serial numbers of known criminal cash. Such a system reflected the financial system in 1980, with the preponderance for using cash in most transactions.

For the context of domestic terrorism in Europe, the objective behind the Recommendation was to identify and confiscate the profits from crimes committed by terrorist groups and to support national counterterrorism efforts. This Recommendation was the first European document to address money laundering, with its concern over the transfer of the proceeds of crime between countries "and the process by which they are laundered" (Council of Europe 1980: 1). In contrast to the US, the first European concern with money laundering was not with organized crime and the proceeds of illegal drug trafficking but with the criminal proceeds of extortion, kidnapping and robbery used to finance terrorism. Nonetheless, the Recommendation of the CoE was ahead of its time in 1980 and would be neither "widely accepted nor implemented" by the member states (Alldridge 2003: 96).

A further challenge during this time was the fact that non-European terrorist groups were also raising funds in Europe. Other groups received support from sympathizers among their diasporas, as well as conducting activities to directly raise money. The Liberation Tigers of Tamil Eelam (LTTE), or simply the Tamil Tigers, for example, had a major role in the movement of heroin from Southeast Asia to Europe. During the 1980s, the number of Tamils involved in drug trafficking in Switzerland meant that the Swiss police focused their efforts on this so-called "Tamil Connection". In addition, the LTTE received significant financial support, both voluntarily and involuntarily, from Tamil communities throughout Europe, the Middle East and North America (Williams 2008: 138–9). According to Vivek Chadha, the LTTE was "neutralised" in the end largely because of "the blocking of its European funding sources", which reduced its operational capacity (Chadha 2015: 28, n.19).

In addition to attacks by the domestic European terrorist groups in the 1970s and 1980s, in the 1990s transnational terrorists were increasingly operating in Europe (Wilkinson 2009).[8] One transnational terrorist plot stands out for the role played by terrorist financing in exposing it before the attack could be completed.[9] In late 2000 a group of four Algerians based in Frankfurt, Germany, were tasked with bombing the Christmas Market in Strasbourg, France, on New Year's Eve. Cross-border police cooperation exposed the plot and prevented the attack. In Germany, police had the group under surveillance after tracking weapons smuggled in from Belgium (Nesser 2015: 94–5), yet it was financing that provided the vital clue that gave the German police enough evidence to arrest the group and seize its weapons and material on 26 December 2000. The clue was not revealed by tracking financial transactions or any of the other techniques promoted by the FATF AML/CFT guidance. Rather, it was the group's need for additional, last-minute funding that led them to call their contact in London requesting more money. That individual was under surveillance by the British security services, who listened to the call requesting more money with its announcement that the group intended to carry out the attack before the end of the year. Details of the call were passed to German authorities, giving them the remaining evidence needed to authorize the raid that led to the arrest and conviction of those involved in the plot (Harris, Wazir & Connolly 2002; *The Guardian* 2003). This case highlights the point that while financial resources are vital to the terrorist group, that does not mean that financial intelligence and CFT measures alone can defeat terrorism.

Northern Ireland

The CoE Recommendation in 1980 sought to address the cross-border movement of funds used to support domestic terrorist groups in Europe. Subsequently, in the UK, the government added the financing dimension to its anti-terrorism legislation in 1989. It serves as one example of national efforts in Europe to tackle terrorist finance, in this case that of British efforts against the IRA within the territory of the UK. The Prevention of Terrorism Act passed through several iterations, beginning in 1974. Measures to address "Financial Assistance for Terrorism" were introduced in 1989 as part of the Prevention of Terrorism (Temporary Provisions) Act 1989. The Act, and most especially this part of it, was concerned solely with the Troubles in Northern Ireland and financial support to "acts of terrorism connected with the affairs of Northern Ireland". One contemporary account of the legislation described the concern over "terrorist money laundering" (Ross 1991: 78). Yet the legislation also only covered the activities of the IRA and Irish National Liberation Army (INLA), while none of the loyalist paramilitaries involved in the Troubles in the 1980s were listed in it (Ross 1991).[10]

As with the other terrorist groups in Europe, the nationalist and loyalist paramilitaries in Northern Ireland were financed by a mixture of contributions and criminal conduct. Even though loyalist groups were not listed in the British legislation they also engaged in criminal financing (Jupp & Garrod 2019). One recent study of the IRA analysed primary archival research, anonymous interviews, published memoirs and the existing academic literature to build a comprehensive view of the financing behind it (Woodford & Smith 2018). The article iterated the various sources and methods employed to raise money in support of the political wing (Sinn Féin), as well as its violent actions. In addition to support from the Irish diaspora (especially in the northeastern US, discussed further below), the IRA raised money through ownership of taxis, "illegal drinking clubs", extortion, kidnapping, robbery and smuggling (Woodford & Smith 2018: 217–22). Among the different sources of funding, smuggling was significant, both across the border to the Republic of Ireland (to arbitrage differences in prices and taxes) as well as into Northern Ireland from the rest of the world. Because of the high taxes imposed on tobacco products in the UK and Ireland, cigarette smuggling was and remains especially lucrative. A report in the *Financial Times* in 2013 suggested that cigarette smuggling continues to be a source of funding for dissident nationalist groups that have not accepted the 1998 Good Friday Agreement (Smyth 2013).

While Woodford and Smith (2018) critique the existing literature on the size of the role attributed to the Irish-American diaspora to finance the IRA, the case documents the utility of diaspora funding in support of political violence at home.[11] At the same time, financial support for the IRA coming from the US was a persistent point of criticism made against the US government. There was a perception that at the federal, state and local levels very little action was taken to prevent fundraising on behalf of the IRA by Irish-Americans.[12] In particular were the collections made by the Irish Northern Aid Committee (NORAID), which ostensibly were for humanitarian purposes but were occasionally diverted to purchase weapons. Collection cups could be found, for example, at shops and pubs in the greater Boston, Massachusetts, area, and while amounts varied year to year, the estimated annual contribution from NORAID was $300,000 (Woodford & Smith 2018: 218).[13]

There is also perhaps some selective amnesia among US CFT professionals concerning the nature and destination of terrorist financing activity in the US before al Qaida became the focus of their attention (discussed later). The literature on terrorism focused more on non-US groups and activities, with little consideration of the potential for terrorist financing by US citizens. More generally, as Woodford and Smith (2018) observe, the literature on the IRA provides some discussion of its financing mechanisms, but the literature on terrorist financing (particularly since 2001) offers "only sporadic references" to the IRA (Woodford & Smith 2018: 215).[14] It may be the case that the story that money from the Irish-American diaspora was the major source for the IRA was accepted without question while other terrorist groups were relying on state sponsors. It was recognized at the time that Irish-Americans were providing financial and material support to the IRA in Northern Ireland. Nonetheless, support from the US continued in some fashion until 2001. Following the 2001 terrorist attacks in the US it became increasingly difficult to support Sinn Féin because it implied support for political violence similar to that of al Qaida (Cochrane 2007: 225–8).

The FARC experience

The case of the Fuerzas Armadas Revolucionarias de Colombia (FARC, Revolutionary Armed Forces of Colombia) is included here for two reasons. First, the organization controlled territory in Colombia and, similar to the experience of IS across the countries of Iraq and Syria (see Chapter 6), controlling territory provides additional sources of funding. Vittori (2011) extended the concept of terrorist financing to be "terrorist resourcing" in her analysis. This approach provides a mechanism by which to include material resources explicitly alongside financial resources for the purpose of analysing the composition and capabilities across a scale of terrorist actors. In turn, the analysis reveals ways to counter these disparate forms of terrorists, from the individual lone actor up to large-scale forces, such as FARC, Hamas and Hezbollah. Her typology extends beyond state sponsors, donations and criminality to incorporate the terrorist group that controls territory, called a "shell state" because it possesses some of the resources normally available to a territorial state (Vittori 2011: 8, 135). For an insurgent or terrorist group, these resources include a population and economy that can be taxed and natural resources or manufacturing facilities that can be exploited. Naturally, controlling territory means that the group can establish a sanctuary space for training and protecting its members.

The second reason to discuss FARC is that by controlling territory and all trade passing through it, the group became involved in coca cultivation and processing coca into cocaine. Yet it is important to recognize that FARC did not set out to become a dominant player in illegal drugs trafficking out of Latin America. Rather, FARC emerged in 1964 as a response to Colombian domestic politics and conflicts over land ownership. It developed as a guerrilla struggle for land re-distribution in support of the peasant farmers of Colombia (Molano 2000: 26–7). In the Cold War context this agenda, combined with its links to the

Communist Party of Colombia, framed the situation as a Marxist insurgency. But in order to maintain support from the people farming in the areas under its control, FARC compromised on coca cultivation, permitting it as a means to address the economic hardship experienced by the farmers. At the same time, it was a policy that provided FARC with substantial financial support through taxation of the coca growers and the cocaine traffickers (Molano 2000: 26–7; Norman 2018: 645–6). Moreover, FARC's revolutionary goals led it to cooperate with other groups, including the IRA, which provided weapons and explosives training in Colombia.

On 8 October 1997, FARC was one of the first groups designated by the US government as a "foreign terrorist organization", in compliance with legislation requiring such a list (Eckert 2008: 212).[15] It was described in the annual State Department *Country Reports on Terrorism* as "Latin America's oldest, largest, and best-equipped terrorist organization" (Bureau of Counterterrorism 2020: 295–6). Yet, while FARC may have been Latin America's oldest insurgent group, the listing as a terrorist group in 1997 paralleled its increased involvement in cocaine production and trafficking (Norman 2018: 649–52). A few years later, an analysis on the importance of Colombia for US foreign and security policy in Latin America observed that "U.S. policy toward Colombia has been driven to a large extent by counter-narcotics considerations, but the situation in that South American country is a national security as much as a drug policy problem" (Rabasa & Chalk 2001: iii). The focus placed on FARC, and the extensive military and economic aid provided to Colombia, was driven by a goal to stop cocaine imports to the US.

Research on FARC's finances, however, drawing on captured documents, reveals that cocaine trafficking was not their leading source of revenue, despite the attention given to it by the US government. Rabasa and Chalk (2001) cited a Colombian government briefing for data on the substantial criminal economy attributed to "guerrillas and paramilitaries" in 1998. A total of $1,098 million was comprised of $551 million from drug trafficking, $311 million from extortion and $236 million from kidnappings (Rabasa & Chalk 2001: 32). Data specific to FARC in 2003 from a study produced by a specialist unit within the Colombian Finance Ministry gave the group a total income of $83.2 million. This income came from kidnapping, $40.3 million; cattle rustling, $24million; drug trafficking, $17 million; bank robberies, $1.2 million; and extortion, $0.7 million (Chernick 2007: 71–4). As Marc Chernick pointed out in his analysis, FARC was not the major illegal drugs cartel implied in media reports. In particular, it was never structured like a drug cartel, having remained organized as a hierarchically structured insurgent army until the peace settlement (Chernick 2007: 71; Norman 2018: 652–3). Overall, while illegal drugs trafficking was a significant concern for external actors (e.g. the US), these other sources of revenue had a greater impact domestically in Colombian society. Kidnapping in particular was widespread and one author described the situation in Colombia as having "acquired industrial proportions" (Sanín 2006: 141). In addition to the $236 million raised in 1998, FARC, together with the Ejército de Liberación Nacional (ELN, National Liberation Army), was thought to be responsible for 20–30 per cent of all kidnappings in the world (Rabasa & Chalk 2001: 32).

The overall conclusion from the case of FARC is that while controlling territory affords a terrorist group additional sources of revenue, those sources are likely not sufficient on their own. It is no longer a matter of raising enough revenue to train, prepare and equip a team for a specific terrorist attack. For the terrorist group that controls territory, it comes with the responsibilities and costs associated with maintaining and retaining that control.

Al Qaida in East Africa and the initial discussion of terrorist financing at the FATF

The end of the Cold War following the fall of the Berlin Wall in 1989 has been identified as a demarcation point in the role of state-sponsored terrorism. In their exploration of a "Political Economy of Terrorism Financing", Jeanne Giraldo and Harold Trinkunas emphasize that the end of the Cold War had an impact beyond the end of proxy conflicts supported by the Soviet Union and the US. Specifically, it unleashed globalization, which allowed for faster and easier cross-border finance supported by the growth of the internet and the spread of mobile phone technology (Giraldo & Trinkunas 2007a: 8–11). Just as globalization unleashed economic growth in the legal economy, it provided terrorist groups with the means to replace the decline of state sponsorship. Yet beyond the state-sponsor dimension of terrorist financing in the twentieth century, a shift in the focus or nexus of cause for terrorism was also observed. The purpose of many terrorist groups in the 1960s and 1970s was political, often to achieve self-determination from a central government or to change the politics of the country by changing the government. In the 1980s and 1990s, however, the cause motivating a terrorist group was increasingly religious rather than ideological, though still with a political purpose and intent (Medd & Goldstein 1997). And with the recognition of a decline in state-sponsored terrorism emerged a realization that a shift to targeting the other sources of financing behind terrorist groups was needed.

The 1993 World Trade Center bombing may have highlighted a transnational terrorist threat against the US, but it was not sufficient to focus attention on terrorist financing. The Director of the FBI noted in the 1999 Senate

Committee hearing that while there had been no further "foreign-directed terrorism" in the US, there had been a number of attacks and disrupted plots against US citizens and property in Asia and the Middle East (Committee on Appropriations 1999: 45–6). The purpose for that Senate hearing was to assess ongoing US government efforts against transnational terrorism and it followed al Qaida's coordinated suicide car bombs targeting the US embassies in Nairobi, Kenya and Dar es Salaam in Tanzania on 7 August 1998. In Nairobi 213 people were killed and over 5,000 injured, while in Dar es Salaam 11 were killed and 77 injured (RDWTI 2009). The challenge at this time was the limited scope and availability of tools to combat the financing of these terrorist groups. As already discussed, in Europe the issue was handled on a national basis, and the situation was the same in the US. The Clinton Administration utilized the Anti-Terrorism and Effective Death Penalty Act (1996) to list foreign terrorist organizations. The government could then block fund transfers involving the listed groups "in the United States" (Committee on Appropriations 1999: 46). Al Qaida was not listed as a foreign terrorist organization until after the US embassy bombings, and its fundraising activities were outside of US territory (Roth, Greenburg & Wille 2004: 32). And the limited attention given to terrorist financing was reflected in the Grand Jury indictment charging Osama bin Laden with the US embassy bombings in 1998. A news report on the indictment mentions the "use of private relief groups 'as a conduit for transmitting funds' for Al Qaeda" (Weiser 1998: n.p.).

The Clinton Administration also pursued international measures to address terrorist financing. At the UN there was the Convention on terrorist financing and Security Council Resolution 1267 (1999) and Security Council Resolution 1333 (2000). Financial sanctions were imposed on the Taliban in Afghanistan to force them to turn over Osama bin Laden "to appropriate authorities in a country where he has been indicted" (Security Council Resolution 1267 (1999): 2, para 2). These sanctions and demands were reiterated in the subsequent Security Council Resolution, along with the freezing of assets of Osama bin Laden "and individuals and entities associated with him" (Resolution 1333 (2000): 4, para 8 (c)). At the FATF in 1999, the US delegation made a presentation suggesting that it could be possible to extend existing AML legislation to include terrorist financing. This led the FATF member state experts to study methods and practices of terrorist financing and report back the following year. Of particular concern was whether the distinction between legal and illegal sources affected the utility of applying AML legislation to terrorist financing. This distinction, the legal money/illegal money dichotomy, was discussed in Chapter 1, along with the fact that intentionality is pivotal to the definition of terrorist financing in the UN Convention. In 2000, the FATF experts agreed that terrorist financing is a serious crime, but disagreed on whether AML legislation could be enforced against it. Where the terrorist group was involved in crime, then the laws against those crimes, including money laundering, would certainly apply. But where the money in possession of the terrorist group did not come from criminal activity, such as donations from the group's supporters, then AML legislation, in some jurisdictions, would not apply because there was no underlying criminal activity behind the funds.

3
IN THE AFTERMATH OF 9/11

For a time after 2001 a frequent approach for introducing the topic of terrorist financing was to relate the announcement of Executive Order 13224 in the White House Rose Garden on 24 September 2001.[1] The "Executive Order on Terrorist Financing: Blocking Property and Prohibiting Transactions With Persons Who Commit, Threaten to Commit, or Support Terrorism" marks the emergence of a more robust and aggressive CFT regime. Along with establishing terrorist financing as the initial battlefront in the US Administration's "Global War on Terror", the "Rose Garden" speech of President George W. Bush provided several refrains that would be repeated regularly (Bush 2001: n.p.). These common quotations included:

> Today, we have launched a strike on the financial foundation of the global terror network.

> We have developed the international financial equivalent of law enforcement's "Most Wanted" list. And it puts the financial world on notice. If you do business with terrorists, if you support or sponsor them, you will not do business with the United States of America.

> We will lead by example. We will work with the world against terrorism. Money is the lifeblood of terrorist operations. Today, we're asking the world to stop payment.

But recall that the US was not one of the four states that had ratified the International Convention for the Suppression of the Financing of Terrorism in 2001. This situation was raised in the Rose Garden speech and President Bush said that he would be asking the Senate to ratify the Convention (which was recorded by the UN as 26 June 2002).

Many of the people living in Europe and North America on 11 September 2001 will have strong memories of that day and the live news reports they may have watched. It is, however, a very Western-centric view of the events.

While suggesting the attacks had global significance, David Lyon reminds us of the Western-centric nature of the narrative surrounding the destruction of the World Trade Center. "True, their perceived significance differs from place to place. For instance, the national daily newspaper in Zambia granted only a couple of column inches of an inside page to the 9/11 attacks, on September 13" (Lyon 2003: 3). Nonetheless, the Western-centric view of terrorism, and terrorist financing, dominated the agenda of the UN, the FATF and other organizations in the first decade of the twenty-first century. It reflects the singular focus of Americans on the 11 September attacks as the seminal and representative example of a terrorist event. Richard English, on the other hand, points out that it was a non-representative, unique event that has not been replicated (English 2016: 142). Nonetheless, for the development of the international regime against terrorist financing, these attacks mark a pivotal moment in the growth and dispersion of CFT. For some authors those terrorist attacks in New York City and Washington, DC marked the beginning of a "global war on terror".

This chapter presents the evolution of CFT in the US, European Union (EU) and at the FATF in the aftermath of 9/11. The first section outlines the US response with CFT legislation, followed by a section presenting the legislation introduced in the EU. The measures introduced in the US and Europe are reflected in the Special Recommendations promulgated by the FATF for international implementation, and are discussed in the third section. The financing methods identified as being used by al Qaida led to an expansion of CFT beyond the AML model, and this is discussed in the fourth section. The final section for this chapter explores the controversy surrounding the surveillance introduced on international financial transactions by the US, with the cooperation of the EU.

The US response and the USA PATRIOT Act

One perspective on the development of the new CFT regime in September 2001 is provided by John B. Taylor, noted economist and, between 2001 and 2005, Under Secretary for International Affairs in the Department of the Treasury. His memoirs for this time in the Bush Administration are titled *Global Financial Warriors: The Untold Story of International Finance in the Post-9/11 World* (Taylor 2007). Much of the book addresses other aspects of his role in government beyond the establishment of a campaign against terrorist financing, such as efforts to reform the International Monetary Fund and the World Bank and, following the invasions of Afghanistan and Iraq, the work to reconstruct their financial systems. The opening chapter, "The First Shot in the Global War on Terror", however, covers the work behind the creation of Executive Order 13224, a Treasury Department unit whose specific purpose was to focus on terrorist financing and the establishment of a surveillance programme that attempts to identify terrorist financing within international financial transactions (discussed further in the last section). The initial work with the Executive Order was to freeze and seize the assets of any identified terrorist and terrorist group, the first named to an ever-growing list that would be replicated by other states and at the UN (CFT at the UN is discussed in Chapter 4).

The work of the Treasury Department as described by Taylor was only one aspect of the US response to expand its CFT capabilities. He also briefly mentions the work of the FBI and Central Intelligence Agency (CIA) to track and trace the money flowing to terrorist groups (Taylor 2007: 24). There was only one reference to the USA PATRIOT Act (at p. 214 because it expanded the "emergency powers" of the president), which arguably had a much greater impact on society than implied by this single reference. The full name of the legislation producing this acronym is Uniting and Strengthening America by Providing Appropriate Tools Required to Intercept and Obstruct Terrorism (USA PATRIOT) Act of 2001. It was introduced to the House of Representatives on 23 October and passed on 24 October, then considered and passed by the US Senate on 25 October before being signed into law by the president on 26 October 2001.[2] The extraordinarily rapid passage of this 131-page legislative document meant that it was largely unread when considered by the House and Senate, an issue that would be raised in subsequent years.

Crucially, the terrorist financing sections of the legislation substantially consists of draft legislation revived from the previous Clinton Administration (Clunan 2006: 592). The legislation involved AML measures, and Title III of the USA PATRIOT Act, "International Money Laundering Abatement and Antiterrorist Financing Act of 2001", reflects that AML orientation. For example, Section 302(a), the Findings of Congress, lists various AML concerns and links them to terrorism by association: "(2) money laundering, and the defects in financial transparency on which money launderers rely, are critical to the financing of global terrorism and the provision of funds for terrorist attacks". As Clunan points out, AML measures are designed to identify and track large quantities of money, the proceeds of illegal drugs trafficking (Clunan 2006: 593). This contrasts with the relatively small sums collected and transferred in support of terrorism (Biersteker & Eckert 2008: 6–7). Moreover, the previous attempt to freeze the assets of al Qaida following the 1998 embassy bombings failed because they were "dispersed and commingled with legitimate humanitarian donations" (Clunan 2006: 594; see also, Roth, Greenburg & Wille 2004: 37–8).

Whereas the expanded scope of AML measures achieved by the USA PATRIOT Act may not have been particularly suitable to identify terrorist financing, they do successfully deal with other forms of criminal finance. Among the additions to the AML regime in the US were foreign corruption as a money laundering offence (Sec. 315); increased customer identification obligations placed on the financial sector (Sec. 312, Sec. 326, Sec. 328); and the expansion of the definition of "financial institution", bringing into the scope of AML/CFT regulations anyone "who engage[s] as a business in the transmission of funds" (Sec. 359). Foreign corruption investigations were soon underway following the creation of a federal task force investigating cases of foreign money laundering (Lichtblau 2003). Similarly, the requirement for increased customer identification checks led to extra work for financial institutions and the growth of an industry sector to help with this workload. The approach was not so much to help confirm the prospective (or continuing) customer's identity as to verify that the customer was not on the list of proscribed terrorists. The recognition and inclusion of the money service business (MSB) as a financial institution for reporting purposes is important. The investigations into terrorist financing exposed the government and its regulatory agencies to unfamiliar mechanisms of money transfer.[3] Yet *hawala* (discussed in more detail later) and other forms of informal value transfer had been discussed by the FATF in its 1996 group of experts meeting as one of a number of non-bank financial institutions.[4] The focus at the time, however, was on the use of alternative remittance or informal value transfer services (IVTSs) for money laundering, predominantly in Asia and the Middle East, and not for terrorist financing.

Following 9/11 the focus shifted and the range of MSB activities was now an area of concern for terrorist financing. The scope of the MSB definition used by the US government covers financial services offered by non-bank companies, and potentially by an individual, "whether or not on a regular basis or as an organized business concern".[5] Of the six services listed within the definition, five have a requirement for a minimum of $1,000 per person per day in transactions to qualify as an MSB. These five services are currency dealer/exchange; cheque cashing; issuer of money orders, travellers' cheques or stored value instruments; seller/redeemer of money orders, travellers' cheques or stored value instruments; and the US Postal Service. The sixth service, money transmitter, is considered an MSB without any requirement of a minimum amount for daily transactions. The FATF definition is similar for the "money or value transfer service", which involves accepting cash, cheques or stored value instruments, and then transferring that value to be paid to the beneficiary. "Sometimes these services have ties to particular geographic regions and are described using a variety of specific terms, including *hawala, hundi,* and *fei-chen.*"[6] The MSB/IVTS known as *hawala* is discussed further in the section entitled "Spreading the net" because of the substantial attention given to it since 2001 and the role of the IVTS in global flows of migrant remittances.

Analysis of financial records for those involved in the 9/11 attacks found that it cost between $400,000 and $500,000 (Roth, Greenburg & Wille 2004: 3). Given this amount of money and the fact that the Clinton Administration attempted to introduce stronger AML/CFT measures comparable to the USA PATRIOT Act, could these stronger measures have caught the financing behind the hijackers? The simple answer is "no", there was nothing about their use of wire transfers and bank accounts considered out of the ordinary for foreign students in the US (Roth, Greenburg & Wille 2004: 133–4, 140–41). If the transactions did not raise any flags, and the wire transfers "were essentially invisible in the billions of dollars in wire transfers that take place every day", then how is the CFT regime going to reveal the future terrorist plot (Roth, Greenburg & Wille 2004: 135)? Some of the tools that emerged to help financial institutions can reveal a network of relationships in the financial system. But the starting point for building the network remains the "person of interest" from which to begin the data search. As seen with the Strasbourg Christmas Market plot discussed in Chapter 2, human intelligence on a potential terrorist suspect is the key to unlocking the picture revealed by the data collected in the CFT regime.

The National Commission on Terrorist Attacks upon the United States was tasked with preparing "a full and complete account" of the 2001 terrorist attacks, including preparedness of government services for these events and how those services responded to the event.[7] The final report of the Commission is 585 pages long, covering terrorism in a broad sense, al Qaida as a terrorist organization, and how to prepare for and prevent future terrorist attacks, as well as covering the 11 September attacks themselves (National Commission on Terrorist Attacks upon the United States 2004). As part of the investigation commission members looked at information on all aspects of the funding behind these attacks and for al Qaida more generally. Some of that analysis is included in the main report, and it is also published in more depth as a separate document, the *Monograph on Terrorist Financing* (National Commission on Terrorist Attacks upon the United States 2004: 169–72, 185–6, 382–3; Roth, Greenburg & Wille 2004). The monograph discusses the sources of money found to be supporting al Qaida before 2001, and addresses sources that were thought to have provided money but for which there was no substantive, verifiable evidence. Among the unveri-fied sources of funding behind al Qaida were unsubstantiated claims that Osama bin Laden possessed and used a considerable personal fortune and that al Qaida had been involved in illegal drugs trafficking or trafficking conflict diamonds. In fact, the family finances given to bin Laden were never that substantial and he had been effectively cut off from the family inheritance in 1994. And beyond the support provided by the Taliban while resident in Afghanistan, al Qaida was not state-sponsored (Roth, Greenburg & Wille 2004: 4, 17, 20, 22–4, 34–5).

The *Monograph on Terrorist Financing* confirmed the involvement of major donors and the use of charities to raise funds. The donors and charities, however, may not have known the ultimate destination and purpose for the money they contributed. Recall the language of the terrorist financing definition in the UN Convention. Terrorist financing is providing funds with the knowledge or intention that they be used for an act of terrorism. With the unaware contributor, the challenge is requiring charities to know where their aid is going and what it is to be used for in that location. It requires a variation on the "know your customer" obligation placed on financial firms for the non-profit sector.[8] The role of charities in funding al Qaida focused more attention on them, which is discussed further in the "Spreading the net" section. The source of funding for a terrorist group is one dimension of the CFT regime, while the other dimension focuses on the method used to move the money. Again, the 9/11 terrorists used the ordinary methods common to any foreign student studying in the US.

There is one further point to highlight from the Rose Garden speech and President Bush's description of terrorist finance as the "lifeblood of terrorist operations". It is a faulty analogy, suggesting that if only countries could stop the financing of terrorism, then they could stop the terrorist group itself. It is a claim that minimizes the political goals of the group engaged in these acts of terrorism and the issues that motivate them and their supporters. The fact that individuals and small groups increasingly finance themselves, through whatever legal and illegal means available, demonstrates the challenge facing the CFT regime to eliminate this so-called "lifeblood" element. The EU also struggled with the problem of self-funded terrorist cells, and its experience with strengthening the CFT regime for the Member States was similar to that of the US, as explained in the next section.

The European Union's parallel response

The experience in Europe of addressing terrorist finance in the late twentieth century was discussed in Chapter 2. Beyond the attempt at the CoE in 1980 to introduce the Recommendation involving terrorist financing, the European members of the G7 contributed to the creation of the FATF in 1989 and the UN Convention in 1999. Following the publication of the first version of the Forty Recommendations in 1990 the European Commission introduced the first EU Directive on money laundering. The 1991 Directive applied to all Member States and the additional states belonging to the European Economic Area. The scope of the Directive allowed states to establish stricter measures than those that were called for within it when they transposed the Directive into national legislation (Gilmore 2011: 222–3). The first revision of the FATF Forty Recommendations in 1996 led to a second money laundering Directive in 1999, which was subjected to debate and delays before it was approved in December 2001. It should be immediately clear from that approval date that it was the impetus of the terrorist attacks in the US that overcame the disagreement of the European Parliament with the European Commission and European Council over the scope of the Directive. The Parliament had been resisting two significant changes introduced by the second Directive to expand the coverage of the AML regime. The first change was the move to include the illegal proceeds generated from a range of serious crimes beyond simply illegal drugs trafficking. It was the second issue, however, that was the main barrier to reaching agreement from Parliament on the second Directive. The proposed text for the Directive added several non-financial businesses to the list of those required to report suspicious transactions, including the legal profession. It was the view of Parliament that to include lawyers was to create the potential for human rights violations because it would contravene the client's right to confidentiality in their dealings with a lawyer (Gilmore 2011: 229–30).[9] These two issues were set aside in the context of a desire to act against terrorist financing in late 2001, even though the second Directive did not explicitly include measures against terrorist financing.

Expanding the scope of the AML regime in Europe before 2001 faced some of the same obstacles and resistance seen in the US at the time. Yet the Second Money Laundering Directive remained substantially the same text as first introduced in 1999, and it did not include the new guidance against terrorist financing released by the FATF in October 2001. Then, in 2003, the FATF published another revision to the core Forty Recommendations along with updated interpretive notes for implementing the guidance. The third EU Directive against money laundering, and now terrorist financing, included seven of the Special Recommendations as well as the revised Forty Recommendations. The FATF's Special Recommendation on wire transfers was addressed under the EU Payments Regulation.[10] And the final Special Recommendation concerning cash couriers, which was introduced in 2004, is also covered by a separate Regulation.[11] The EU legal system treats a Regulation differently from a Directive. Directives are binding legislation but they must first be transposed into national legislation. Regulations, on the other hand, are binding legislation that are applicable as written in all Member States on the implementation date, independent of national legislation (Shaw 2000: 243–5). The legal nature of the EU and the separate, national obligations of its Member States under international treaties and UN membership introduced complexities to the EU CFT regime, which may limit its effectiveness.[12]

There were fundamental differences between the EU and the US in the organization and application of initial CFT measures in late 2001 (Clunan 2006: 580–82). The USA PATRIOT Act, for example, was not replicated, though similar expanded AML measures were included in the second Directive. Moreover, there were differences in the enforcement of asset freezing sanctions, with some EU Member States recognizing the human rights deficiencies in the implementation of these sanctions. Several of these differences in the EU with the introduction of international CFT measures are discussed further below. The controversy surrounding US surveillance and data collection of wire transfers from SWIFT, a company headquartered in Europe, is discussed in the last section of this chapter. The European court cases challenging the imposition of UN asset freezing sanctions on individuals and groups accused of terrorist financing are discussed in Chapter 4. Beyond these differences, the AML/CFT regime of the EU continued to evolve. The sixth Directive on money laundering and terrorist financing was promulgated on 23 October 2018, with an implementation date by the Member States before 3 December 2020.[13]

FATF response: Special Recommendations on Terrorist Financing

As mentioned previously, Taylor, in his memoirs, described the creation of a unit in the US Treasury Department charged with directing its efforts against terrorism. This team tracked all available data on asset freezes by country, helped to coordinate with other countries when the US released an updated list of the individuals and groups whose financial assets should be frozen, and "developed and implemented international standards" (Taylor 2007: 17–19). This work on developing international standards included the production of the initial eight Special Recommendations on Terrorist Financing that would be agreed by FATF members at an extraordinary meeting held in Washington, DC on 29–30 October 2001. To support the implementation of these new Special Recommendations the FATF prepared a self-assessment questionnaire for members and other states to determine their level of compliance. The self-assessment procedure would also identify the areas where change was needed to become compliant. Additionally, information came from the report of the November 2001 typologies meeting of experts, which claimed to be "the first time" terrorist financing was discussed by the group. As with the report from the December 2000 meeting, this report's discussion includes example cases of possible terrorist financing to demonstrate what governments should look out for when investigating terrorism cases.

The first Special Recommendation re-enacted the strategy from the first Recommendation of the original Forty Recommendations. In keeping with its focus on the money laundering from illegal drugs, the first version of the Forty Recommendations called on states to ratify and implement the 1988 Vienna Convention against illegal drugs trafficking "without further delay".[14] In 2001, the first Special Recommendation directed states to "take immediate steps" for the ratification and implementation of the 1999 Convention for the Suppression of the Financing of Terrorism along with implementing all relevant UN Security Council Resolutions. It represented a crucial first step for establishing an effective international regime against terrorist financing, given the very small number of states that had ratified the treaty by September 2001.

Special Recommendation II addressed the issue raised at the FATF typologies meeting in 2000 concerning the fact that in some legal systems AML legislation would not apply to terrorist financing. It directs states to explicitly criminalize terrorist groups, acts of terrorism and the financing of terrorism. It also recommends that AML legislation be amended to add these new terrorism offences as predicate crimes[15] for money laundering. The interpretive note for this Special Recommendation provides more detailed information on the definitions and characteristics of terrorism, terrorists and acts of terror.

The third Special Recommendation brings the practice of freezing and seizing the assets of anyone accused of terrorist financing, from the White House Rose Garden speech, into FATF guidance, as directed by UN Security Council Resolutions. This practice at the Security Council was contentious and challenged in national courts by some of those whose financial accounts were frozen. The use of these targeted financial sanctions is explored in Chapter 4.

The importance of suspicious transaction reports (STRs) is re-emphasized with Special Recommendation IV, which directs that STRs are submitted when terrorist financing is suspected. The usefulness of this additional reporting requirement is questionable because of the variable nature of national STR reporting regimes and the quality of the data provided in a report (Chaikin 2009). Consider, for example, the reporting of STRs in the US (where they are known as suspicious activity reports, SARs). In 2020, there were a total of 2,504,511 reports submitted by a range of financial and non-financial firms. The large number of reports requiring analysis for the reported activity provides a challenge, giving some benefit to the "Suspicious Activity Category/Type" field in the report. The "Terrorist Financing" category was used in 1,907 reports submitted in 2020, a more manageable quantity for investigation.[16] Nonetheless, the quality of reports remains an issue: on what basis was "Terrorist Financing" the category selected rather than any of the many other choices, including "Money Laundering"?

Special Recommendation V is simple and straightforward, calling for international cooperation in support of investigations into terrorist financing, acts of terrorism and terrorist groups. Perhaps there is no interpretive note for this Special Recommendation because it was felt to be straightforward. There are challenges to its implementation, however, because of disagreements between countries as to whether a specific group should in fact be named a terrorist group, and within the EU at least there is also the ability of the group to challenge its designation in court.

As mentioned earlier, investigations into the financing behind terrorism following 9/11 brought previously unfamiliar mechanisms of money transfer to the attention of US government officials. This discovery that not everyone uses a retail bank branch to send money home to family is reflected in Special Recommendation VI. The Recommendation seeks to formalize the informal, directing that states legislate processes to register and monitor alternative remittance or IVTSs. Similarly, the misuse of charities for terrorist financing had also emerged, and Special Recommendation VIII seeks to address the problem of charities serving as a source of terrorist funding or as a conduit for moving money to support a terrorist group. Because of their use by al Qaida these two topics received a lot of attention, and are discussed further in the next section.

The requirement that information about the person sending money must travel as part of the wire transfer message is made in Special Recommendation VII, which in the EU was implemented using a Regulation. This Special Recommendation also expects states to require the money transfer service receiving and processing the wire transfer to conduct suspicious transaction checks if a transfer arrives without the expected details about the sending person. The interpretive note for Special Recommendation VII provides further details on the expectations for its implementation, including identifying several forms of transfer that are exempt and explaining its application for domestic transfers that remain within a single territory.

The final Special Recommendation was introduced in 2004 with the recognition that the actions taken to prevent terrorist financing had encouraged the use of bulk cash couriers to avoid suspicious transaction reporting when moving money across borders. Special Recommendation IX directs states to introduce measures to record and monitor the movement of cash and negotiable instruments across borders. Its interpretive note identifies a reporting threshold and explains that gold and other precious minerals and stones are not covered by it.

After a decade, the distinction for having "Special Recommendations on Terrorist Financing" had declined. They either became out of date (Special Recommendation I) or simply became part of the broader application of financial data surveillance against all forms of criminality, now including the financing of weapons of mass destruction. The 2012 edition of the Forty Recommendations integrated the Special Recommendations that remained relevant into a revised set of 40 comprehensive Recommendations.

Spreading the net: *hawala* and charities

Recall that AML practices began by monitoring and tracking transactions conducted through banks and other financial institutions. They were the first areas identified by the FATF as used for money laundering in 1990. As criminals adjusted to the AML restrictions they turned to other forms of economic transactions to move their money, as reported by the FATF in subsequent typology reports. Yet the use of what are known as "informal" financial practices for money laundering was also recognized from the start and they are part of the information exchanged at the typology meetings. The first point to recognize is the distinction between formal and informal in this context. Banking and other financial services are tightly regulated, to protect customers from fraud and to protect society from the cost of bailing out failed financial institutions. At its most basic, a bank is a financial firm that accepts deposits and lends money, whereas an MSB only accepts money to send it on to someone else or to provide the customer with a money order, prepaid debit card or other negotiable instrument. In most jurisdictions MSBs are also now licensed, but generally not as a bank. Consequently, the informal business in this context is one that is not licensed and regulated as a bank or MSB.[17] Beginning in September 2001, the informal financial practice that received the most attention was *hawala*, the Arabic name for a system that has been operating from South Asia, along the Indian Ocean, to the east coast of Africa for centuries.

The claim that *hawala* is a "banking system built for terrorism", as it was represented by the news media in 2001, is a very modern, Western-centric and ahistorical understanding of money and finance in the world (de Goede 2003: 514; citing Ganguly 2001). It is true that al Qaida used *hawala* while in Afghanistan; everyone in Afghanistan used it because there was no longer a formal banking system functioning in the country (Roth, Greenburg & Wille 2004: 25). This situation became quite clear following the US invasion, leading to the work that was necessary to re-establish a formal banking system (Taylor 2007: 29–69). Meanwhile, non-governmental organizations (NGOs) and aid agencies operating in Afghanistan before and after the invasion also used *hawala* to move money into the country. In the absence of a formal retail bank branch network, or when denied access to a retail bank branch, people turn to whatever methods are available to them for sending money to family and friends, domestically and across borders. The latter point is why these non-bank methods to transfer money continue to operate with success throughout the world; they provide the means for migrant workers to send money home. Knowledge of migrant remittances was just as sparse among government policy-makers as knowledge of *hawala* and other IVTSs. Taylor highlighted his role in establishing a "Global Remittance Initiative" following the discovery that one of the reasons for using *hawala* was its lower cost than using a bank or MSB, combined with the calculations made by his staff that migrant remittances often exceeded the official development assistance received by many destination countries (Taylor 2007: 26–7).[18]

Alongside the fact that migrant remittances comprise a greater sum than official development assistance for many migrant sending countries, it needs to be understood that this sum is the result of a multitude of small transactions. Data from 2018, for example, on the average remittance amount sent home to Colombia from the US was $290, from Spain was $270 and from the rest of South America was $210 (Orozco, Porras & Yansura 2019: 8). The World Bank reported in 2019 that global remittances for 2018 were $529 billion, with a projection for 2019 that global remittances would reach $550 billion. The Covid-19 pandemic has disrupted remittance flows just as it has affected most other areas of life. Fortunately, the expected decline of remittances predicted by the World Bank in April 2020 did not occur. Instead, the World Bank reported in 2021 that global remittances amounted to $540 billion in 2020, a drop of only $8 billion from the $548 billion reported for 2019 (World Bank 2021). The World Bank is reporting data on remittance flows recorded and measured by the reporting agencies. The actual flow will be greater than this reported sum because of the unrecorded flows that continue to use the informal systems that remain outside of government licensing programmes. This remains essentially unchanged from the data collected in the early 2000s, after the reported remittance flows increased significantly as unlicensed businesses were registered and licensed, with states extending their AML/CFT regime to include all forms of MSBs.

The conventional presentation of a modern *hawala* transaction includes a migrant sending money home, a family member receiving the money and, between them, two money service agents (called *hawaladars*) performing the transaction. The migrant provides the amount to be transferred to their local agent with contact details for the recipient. In return, the local agent provides them with a reference number for the receiving family member or acquaintance to use as verification. The local agent contacts an agent at the destination location with details on the amount, the intended recipient and verification code to confirm the identity of the recipient. The destination agent may deliver the funds directly if they have the address to do so, or will wait to be contacted by the recipient. Following confirmation of the verification code, the money is delivered and the transaction complete. This process operates in functionally the same manner across all boundaries for migrant remittances, transfers from the UK to Pakistan, Sweden to Somalia, and from the US to Mexico. What is important to recognize with these transactions is the absence of an actual transfer of currency between the two agents. The process of intermediation and settlement happens locally for each participant in the transaction chain, balancing out between the transactions sent and the transactions received.

The informal money transfer agent may operate alongside any number of other business activities, including at corner shops and travel agents. Nonetheless, as Marieke de Goede (2005) explains, the environment in the aftermath of 9/11 produced a discourse framing *hawala* as part of the domain of criminality. Further, it was consistently contrasted with the safety of Western formal banking systems – her analysis was published before the 2008 financial crisis demolished many perceptions of safety, stability and probity held about the Western financial system (de Goede 2005: 513–5). This discourse may have developed not only from the depiction of *hawala* operating out of dimly lit back offices described in the popular press, but also may have emerged from the American experience with a similar informal system, the Black Market Peso Exchange (BMPE). The BMPE became widely known from its use by Colombian drug cartels to move their profits from the US to Colombia. The story of the BMPE, however, predates the emergence of illegal drug trafficking when it helped Colombian firms work around government capital controls and facilitated migrant remittances from the US to Colombia (Cassara 2015). Evading capital controls is often a criminal offence, but not at the level of terrorism or even illegal drugs-related money laundering. Nonetheless, the perception of explicit criminality was foregrounded, concealing the fact that a substantial use of these informal systems has been the transfer of migrant remittances.

The experience of charities following 9/11 paralleled *hawala* because of their identification as a funding source for al Qaida. The role of charities behind al Qaida was briefly explained in the *Monograph on Terrorist Financing* (Roth, Greenburg & Wille 2004: 21). Released in 2004, its description is more balanced than initial statements about the role of charities in funding the terrorist attacks (Warde 2007: 127–31). In particular, Roth, Greenburg and Wille (2004) highlighted the place of charitable donations as a central element of Islam (as it is in traditional Christianity under the term tithe). Nonetheless, it was also true that charities, knowingly and unknowingly, contributed to al Qaida and have been linked to other terrorist groups. In the feverish environment after 11 September 2001 all Islamic charities were investigated for funding terrorism and, if suspected, their assets were frozen as part of the new financial front against terrorism. Further investigations revealed that for most accusations no connection was found, or in several cases it was only the presence of a trustee for the charity with "suspicious links" to either al Qaeda or Hamas. Consequently, combining this line of logic with the idea of "six degrees of separation" means that practically anyone could plausibly be linked to a terrorist group.

Nonetheless, some charities have been convicted of terrorist financing-related charges, for example the Holy Land Foundation in the US. The US government shut down what had been the largest Islamic charity in the country in December 2001, accusing it of supporting a terrorist organization, specifically Hamas. The first trial ended in a mistrial in 2007, and they were then found guilty at a second trial in 2008 for supporting a terrorist group and money laundering. The argument of the prosecution was that the group was indirectly supporting terrorism, in part because the US had declared Hamas to be a terrorist organization. By providing support to its humanitarian arm, the charity's donations meant that

Hamas's other resources could be used for its militant arm (Milton-Edwards 2017: 171–2).

The particularly problematic nature of the focus placed on Islamic charities in the immediate aftermath of the 2001 terrorist attacks involves the tension that it has created between freedom of expression, that is your freedom to choose what charity to support (which in this instance is related also to freedom of religion), and the desire for security against terrorism. And certainly, given a widespread perception that equates terrorism with Islam, the charitable obligations of the Islamic faithful were perceived as a way to conceal the funding of terrorism (Warde 2007: 145–7). A report released in June 2009 by the American Civil Liberties Union, titled "Blocking Faith, Freezing Charity", documented the impact of CFT measures in the US on the rights of American Muslims to profess their faith and practice their religion through the act of giving to charities. It found that the tactics used by the government were undermining their fundamental human rights, specifically freedom of religion, freedom of association and freedom from discrimination (Turner 2009).

This problem remains a challenge for charities today, in that just as a bank must "know its customer", the charity also must now "know its donors". This situation emerged with the implementation of FATF Special Recommendation VIII, now simply Recommendation 8, which is concerned that non-profit organizations may be "vulnerable to terrorist financing abuse". In the UK, for example, the Charities Commission for England and Wales produced guidance outlining its strategy to prevent any possible misuse of a charity by a terrorist group. This guidance incorporated a compliance toolkit to assist charities in preventing possible misuse, including instructions for due diligence and "knowing" their donors, beneficiaries and partners to avoid any suspicious links (Charities Commission for England and Wales 2016). As a result, charities of all sizes must provide annual accounting reports documenting inflows and outflows for the charity. The level of detail and complexity of the report naturally increases with the size of the charity, based on assets and donations. One further result of the focus placed on charities as possible sources and conduits of terrorist financing was the closure of their bank accounts. The experience of MSBs and charities with account closures and new account rejections is part of a wider phenomenon known as derisking, and it is discussed in more detail in Chapter 5.

North Atlantic controversy: SWIFT and the Terrorist Finance Tracking Programme

The secret use of SWIFT wire transfer data by the US to search for terrorist financing was exposed in 2006. The exposure of this invasion of privacy produced a dispute between Americans and Europeans. Turning once again to *Global Financial Warriors*, here is John Taylor's perspective on the exposure of the US government's secret collection of wire transfer data from SWIFT: "Those of us involved in creating the program in 2001 ... were dismayed and disappointed when information about the program and how it worked was leaked to newspapers", which then published the information even though senior government had requested them not to publish it (Taylor 2007: 20). His claim was that even though terrorists might suspect the existence of the programme, publicly revealing its existence and sharing details of how it worked helped the terrorists. Similarly, the Under Secretary of the Treasury for the Office of Terrorism and Financial Intelligence, stated, following the revelation:

> Until today, we have not discussed this program in public for an obvious reason: the value of the program came from the fact that terrorists didn't know it existed. They may have heard us talking about "following the money," but they didn't know that we were obtaining terrorist-related data from SWIFT. Many may not have even known what SWIFT was.
>
> With today's revelations, this is unfortunately no longer true. This is a grave loss. (Levey 2006)

Sitting in Washington, DC this viewpoint may have been self-evident, however, for a number of people sitting in other cities, and particularly those cities outside of the US, that was not the case. The exposure of the US government's Terrorist Finance Tracking Programme (TFTP) produced a transatlantic tension in international cooperation because this CFT initiative did not comply with norms of privacy prevalent in the EU (Mitsilegas 2014).

SWIFT, formerly known as the "Society for Worldwide Interbank Financial Telecommunication", is the member-owned cooperative providing secure transmission of wire transfer messages between the member financial institutions (Scott & Zachariadis 2012). Consequently, the US government was searching for terrorist-related needles within the massive haystack composed of every other international wire transfer. In 2006 there were, on average, 11.4 million daily transfer messages, for an annual total of over 2.8 billion wire transfer messages. The number of SWIFT wire transfer messages transmitted daily has continued to grow, reaching a daily average of 37.7 million in a total of over 9.5 billion messages in 2020.[19] To be clear, SWIFT is not a repository for all financial transaction data. It processes messages between banks for transfers that cross an international border. These messages contain account details of the sender, account details of the receiver and the amount of money sent. A transfer between accounts completely within one national jurisdiction will normally use a national network connecting financial institutions. Importantly, the SWIFT transfer message provides the identity data that regulators argue is not available when a transaction is processed through an informal transfer system, and which prevents analysis by investigators.

The TFTP was exposed on the front page of *The New York Times* on 23 June 2006, with similar articles published in several other US newspapers, including the *Los Angeles Times*, *The Wall Street Journal* and *The Washington Post* (Lichtblau & Risen 2006). In contrast to the perception that the programme sifted through an immense haystack in search of needles, the Secretary of the Treasury was quoted in one article asserting that this "essential tool" for CFT was "not 'data mining' or trolling through the private financial records of Americans". Rather than being a "fishing expedition", TFTP was "a sharp harpoon aimed at the heart of terrorist activity" (Simpson 2006: n.p.). While this assertion may have mollified concerns held by some US citizens, it did not address the privacy concerns of citizens and officials in Europe. Moreover, while at the time of these revelations TFTP access to SWIFT data was limited, initially, in 2001, the entire database of SWIFT transfer messages was provided to US government analysts. Only later was the potential abuse of completely open access recognized, with the US government then having to request specific data searches for SWIFT to conduct, and then provide the results to the US government (Lichtblau & Risen 2006).

One factor in the trans-Atlantic dimension of the controversy over the TFTP involved the physical structure of the SWIFT network. The cooperative is formally registered and headquartered in Belgium, with an operating centre in the US maintaining a mirror copy of all message traffic to provide a backup for business continuity. This structure was crucial to the establishment of the TFTP as international cooperation was not necessary because the US government could simply serve its administrative subpoenas on the US operating centre (Amicelle 2011: 9). This did not mean that a few officials in Europe were not aware of the programme before the newspaper reports brought it to public attention. Public exposure did, however, bring the TFTP to the attention of European officials responsible for data protection and privacy. They, in turn, criticized the individuals that were aware of the programme for failing to maintain European norms for data protection (Amicelle 2011: 11–13; Associated Press 2006; Bilefsky 2006). "When the programme became public, the ECB and other 'insiders' were interrogated about their complicity in the secret and their (apparent) disregard for data protection rights and civil liberties" (de Goede & Wesseling 2017: 258). Over the next few years, the EU and US negotiated an agreement covering the exchange of SWIFT data for the TFTP while SWIFT redesigned its network architecture to reduce the exposure of EU citizens to American surveillance (Amicelle 2011: 14–19; de Goede 2011). For its part, SWIFT explained the introduction of multiple processing zones, with a new global operating centre in Switzerland, as a move to meet increased customer requirements.[20]

The controversy over the TFTP, as documented in the cited academic analyses, situated it in opposition with the norms of data protection and privacy promoted by the EU. These norms are reflected not only in this instance, but also in the General Data Protection Regulation (GDPR) and its imposition on all online services used by EU citizens within EU jurisdiction.[21] This viewpoint is contradicted, however, by the proposal that emerged for a European TFTP during the negotiations in 2010, permitting the transfer of SWIFT data between the EU and US. At the time of writing the establishment of a European TFTP remains a work in progress, but this has not prevented European access and analysis of data extracted from SWIFT message traffic. Created in 2004, the Privacy and Civil Liberties Oversight Board serves as an oversight mechanism of the TFTP in the US.[22] In 2020 it released a report reviewing the conduct of the TFTP, which included information on cooperation with European officials to extract financial transaction data from SWIFT. In addition to reporting that "more than 80,000 individual leads from TFTP" were shared in the period of January 2016 to November 2018, the report included information following a number of "unclassified examples" of terrorist attacks in Europe (Klein 2020: 2–3). This cooperation had been confirmed by the European Commission in 2019, though the figure they gave was more than 70,000 (European Commission 2019: 7). Clearly it continues to be the case that security (from terrorism) takes precedence over the privacy of the individual in Europe.

4
COLLECTIVE ACTION AGAINST TERRORIST FINANCING

The discussion around the definition of terrorism in Chapter 1 emphasized that it is a form of political violence undertaken with the goal of changing a government policy, or even to change the government itself. And until the late twentieth century terrorism was generally viewed as a problem of domestic politics with few cross-border aspects. This view shifted with the recognition of growing transnational terrorism with cross-border aspects, including the money used to fund the terrorist group. In addition to the Convention on terrorist financing, the UN Security Council has published numerous Resolutions imposing financial sanctions and targeting the money behind specific terrorist groups. But a pivotal Security Council Resolution regarding terrorism and "the inherent right of individual or collective self-defence" was issued on 12 September 2001. The first paragraph of Resolution 1368 reads that the Security Council, "Unequivocally condemns in the strongest terms the horrifying terrorist attacks which took place on 11 September 2001 in New York, Washington, D.C. and Pennsylvania and regards such acts, like any act of international terrorism, as a threat to international peace and security". It continues by expressing sympathy and condolences, calling on all states to seek out not only the perpetrators of these attacks but also to increase efforts to prevent future attacks. Further, it asserts the readiness of the Security Council to combat terrorism in all its forms under the UN Charter. Later that day the Secretary-General of the UN was asked by a reporter what his personal feelings were at the time. The response of Kofi Annan was:

> I cannot describe how I felt yesterday – the shock, the anguish and the realisation that men can be so cruel and so inhuman. To watch what was going on downtown; to see the buildings crumble and see the citizens of this great city scrambling for safety and in one brief moment, all our sense of security was gone. (United Nations Secretary-General 2001)

Before looking at the UN Security Council measures to combat terrorist financing it is helpful to understand the primary tool employed by the Security Council. The next section provides a short review of the evolution of targeted sanctions imposed by the UN. The following section then expands on the use of targeted sanctions in terms of their application against terrorist groups and, specifically, the financing of terrorism. This use of targeted sanctions was resisted by some of the individuals and groups added to the UN sanctions list. The third section discusses several of the legal challenges made against the use of Security Council targeted sanctions in European and national court systems. This litigation motivated further refinement of the practices and procedures employed by the Security Council, and some of these changes are explained in the fourth section. The final section outlines the organizational structures created within the Security Council and the UN system to address terrorism and to coordinate their counterterrorism actions.

Sanctions at the UN: from comprehensive to targeted

One challenge for the UN is the enforcement of its Directives. In a situation that is not a clear issue of international peace and security, the UN is unable to justify the use of military force or the deployment of peacekeepers. The "naming and shaming" by the FATF of countries that fail to implement and enforce its Forty Recommendations is explored in Chapter 5 (Nance 2015). Such an approach operates as a form of "soft law" seeking to persuade compliance, whereas UN sanctions are a more coercive or "hard" approach to force compliance. The fundamental purpose for most sanctions, whether by a single state or by a collection of like-minded states, is to achieve a foreign policy goal. Another purpose is to constrain the actions of a target state, which indirectly may serve to achieve the policy goal (Biersteker, Tourinho & Eckert 2016: 21–2). Sanctions also may be understood as a "signalling" tool in order to demonstrate leadership or to support international standards. Such signalling may be directed at a domestic audience as much as it is directed at a target (foreign) audience. Thus, in the context of the terrorist financing sanctions introduced by the US in September 2001, it must be agreed that they were just as much about signalling action against terrorism to the US domestic audience as they were a tool against the financing of al Qaida. Fundamental to the proposals to impose sanctions is a belief that sanctions serve to demonstrate a firmness of resolve by the state or international organization and its intention to force a change in the policies, actions or conduct of another state or its governing elite, while the sanctions themselves operate as a demonstration that falls short of using military action to *force* or manufacture the desired change (Wallensteen & Staibano 2005). Since the end of the Cold War the Security Council has increasingly used sanctions as the tool to enable and force international action.

At the same time, the imposition of international sanctions has been controversial because of the frequent unintended humanitarian impact. This has motivated an evolution of the sanctions imposed by the UN Security Council. Over time they have changed from the comprehensive economic sanctions placed on an entire country (e.g. Iraq following its invasion of Kuwait in 1990) to the introduction of targeted sanctions against specific named individuals or groups. This evolution was in response to the difficulties experienced with attempts to impose a full embargo on trade while also allowing humanitarian aid to pass, as well as in monitoring to prevent any violation of the sanctions (Staibano 2005). The evolution of sanctions was guided by several initiatives in the late 1990s to clarify and improve the structure of them into "targeted" sanctions. The targeted approach is intended to avoid humanitarian problems created by the use of comprehensive sanctions. Moreover, it should enhance the efficacy of UN-directed sanctions as a tool for achieving international peace and security.

Three major international initiatives, the Interlaken Process, the Bonn-Berlin Process and the Stockholm Process, considered different aspects in the development of targeted sanctions. The Interlaken Process in 1998 explored methods to improve the effectiveness of financial sanctions, producing a manual for practitioners involved in drafting UN Resolutions that contained financial sanctions. The German Foreign Office initiated the second project, the Bonn-Berlin Process, in 1999 to explore ways of improving an interrelated set of sanctions involving travel bans and limitations on aviation and importing weapons. The Stockholm Process then built on the work accomplished by its predecessors and sought to identify further ways of improving the implementation of sanctions. Overall, the goal was to improve the content of UN Resolutions that established sanctions, the implementation procedures undertaken at the national level, and the processes used to monitor and verify enforcement. Later, the work of these projects was consolidated by the Targeted Sanctions Initiative based at the Graduate Institute Geneva, which analysed the effectiveness of targeted sanctions as a tool in support of UN objectives (Eckert, Biersteker & Tourinho 2016).

Targeted sanctions come in several forms, including sanctions against the importation/exportation of arms and munitions, petroleum and fuel, as well as other specific items, such as replacement aircraft parts, tobacco and luxury goods. There can also be travel sanctions that ban foreign travel by the targeted individuals, and financial sanctions that freeze and even seize the foreign assets of individuals, groups and the state (Biersteker, Tourinho & Eckert 2016: 25–7). The logic is that those named in a UN Security Council sanctions resolution possess an essential factor that will be discomfited by the sanctions imposed on them. They have a need or a desire to engage with others beyond the national border and therefore will react to the limitations placed on them by a travel ban or a trade embargo (Wallensteen & Helena 2012). Although targeted sanctions are directed at individuals or groups rather than the country, they remain state-based, or at least state-focused. The sanctions resolution targets individuals that are part of the ruling elite of a state, with an objective to change the policy of the state. This is explicitly not the case when targeting sanctions against individual terrorists and terrorist groups, where the intention then is to limit and constrain terrorist actions rather than to change state policy (Biersteker, Tourinho & Eckert 2016: 20).

Consequently, the application of targeted sanctions against non-state actors is more challenging and, to some extent, it is more difficult to measure success. It is also not as easy to identify a member or associate of a non-state actor to add them to a sanctions list as it is to impose targeted sanctions on the ruling elites of a state. The problem is made more difficult by the fact that terrorist groups will attempt to disguise their membership and all sources of support that they receive from their sympathizers. In the case of the financial sanctions implemented by UN Security Council Resolutions against the individuals and entities believed to be associated with Osama bin Laden and the al Qaida network, a number of individuals and groups were wrongly included. This led, in turn, to the legal challenges made against those sanctions, which are discussed further in the section entitled "Full Court Press against UN sanctions". The use of targeted sanctions against terrorist financing is discussed in the next section.

Introducing targeted sanctions for counterterrorism

The Convention for the Suppression of the Financing of Terrorism provides one international framework for addressing terrorist financing. The limited enthusiasm for ratifying the treaty before September 2001 reflected the general level of concern about terrorism and the financing of terrorism prevalent in many countries at the beginning of the twenty-first century. It had been much the same at the UN as well, where terrorism was viewed as a national problem rather than a problem for international peace and security. Gehring, Dorsch and Dörfler (2019) identify a shift in attitude at the UN Security Council in 1985 changing that perception and now recognizing terrorism as an international problem requiring increased international cooperation in response to terrorist events (119–22). The development of targeted sanctions alongside the shift in understanding of transnational terrorism as a threat to international peace and security led to the Security Council Resolution in 1999 targeting the Taliban in Afghanistan following the East Africa embassy bombings by al Qaida. The central issue that shaped the Security Council's approach to counterterrorism and CFT following the September 2001 terrorist attacks was not the application of targeted sanctions. Rather it was the lack of human rights safeguards in the mechanisms behind the decision to impose targeted sanctions on a specific person (Minnella 2019). Efforts to introduce human rights provisions (and specifically the right to challenge being placed on the list) into the process at the Security Council became a driving force behind the evolution of CFT as practiced by the UN.

Targeted sanctions were introduced against the Taliban by Resolution 1267 (1999) to reinforce earlier Security Council Resolutions regarding the actions of the Taliban in Afghanistan, which represented a threat to international peace and security. This Resolution was introduced under Chapter VII (Action with Respect to Threats to the Peace, Breaches of the Peace, and Acts of Aggression) of the UN Charter, making compliance obligatory for all UN member states. It established a Security Council committee to identify specific targets for the sanctions and to report on their progress and impact (¶6). The initial sanctions imposed were a ban on all aircraft connected to the Taliban and an asset freeze of anyone identified as members or supporters of the Taliban by this committee (¶4). Further, Resolution 1267 demanded that the Taliban "turn over Usama bin Laden without further delay" to face his indictment for the 1998 embassy bombings in East Africa (¶2). The Taliban did not respond to the demands of the UN Security Council, which then expanded the scope of the targeted sanctions with Resolution 1333 in December 2000 to include an arms ban, reduction of diplomatic contact to isolate the Taliban in the international community, an extension of the aviation ban to cover all flights in and out of Taliban-controlled territory, and the freezing of the assets of bin Laden and any individual or group (including al Qaida) associated with him. It also expanded the list established by Resolution 1267 to include any airport providing an aviation link to Taliban-controlled territory, along with the names of bin Laden's associates (¶16). With Resolution 1333 the committee established by Resolution 1267 also became known as the "Al-Qaida and Taliban Sanctions Committee", and one of the foundations for CFT at the UN through the application of targeted sanctions against those accused of financing terrorism.[1]

The expansion of targeted sanctions by Resolution 1333 had little time to have any impact against transnational terrorism originating in Afghanistan. The al Qaida attacks against the US were already in development, and following those attacks in New York City and Washington, DC, the Security Council introduced Resolution 1373. It begins by re-emphasizing the earlier Resolutions' call for the establishment of financial sanctions against terrorism, and specifically the Taliban, Osama bin Laden and al Qaida. The Resolution directs several actions to be taken by UN member states, and like Resolution 1267 it is introduced under

Chapter VII of the UN Charter. The first action is to "prevent and suppress" terrorist financing, to criminalize all activities involved in terrorist financing and to freeze the assets of anyone involved in terrorist financing (¶1). The second section of the Resolution is essentially a ban on state-sponsored terrorism, directing all states to fully support the efforts taken by other states against terrorist financing. The Resolution further reinforced the obligations stated in previous Resolutions, and it directed the establishment of a committee to monitor the implementation of this Resolution. The operations of the Counter-Terrorism Committee (CTC) of the Security Council, alongside the other offices of the UN dealing with terrorist financing, are discussed further in the section entitled "Organizing the UN to counter terrorism".

The expansion of the 1267 sanctions list to include anyone accused of possessing an "association" with bin Laden or al Qaida exposed the unidirectional nature of the listing process. Following the attacks in September 2001 the list grew significantly with the addition of such associates, with many names supplied by the US. Initially member states provided names to the committee without necessarily providing evidence supporting their inclusion on the sanctions list (Minnella 2019: 40–41; Gehring & Dörfler 2013: 574–6). Listed individuals discovered their presence on the sanctions list only once their bank accounts were frozen, leaving them unable to pay their bills, buy food and generally live life. Such was the case of three Somali-Swedes connected to the al Barakaat International Foundation in Sweden after the addition of their names to the sanctions list by the US in November 2001. The court case they brought against the European Commission for unjustly imposing the UN sanctions on them is discussed in the next section. The circumstances in Sweden for these men were that their bank accounts were frozen, yet the government continued to provide welfare payments to them in accordance with Swedish law (Cramér 2003: 91). Beyond these government payments, local citizens were offended by their listing at the UN Security Council and established a "Solidarity Committee" to provide them and their families with additional support. This local committee collected cash donations, avoiding the problem of having a bank account frozen, and because of the large number of small donations made to the committee, Swedish police refused to prosecute them for violating the sanctions (Analytical Support and Sanctions Monitoring Team 2007: 25–6).

At the UN the Swedish delegation petitioned on behalf of its citizens to have their names removed from the list because they were wrongly targeted. This case led Sweden, supported by France, to point out that due process procedures were not followed when adding names to the sanctions list. Sweden's request for evidence that its three citizens were connected to terrorism or terrorist financing from the US resulted in 27 pages of background information about al Barakaat. The material did not, however, contain anything demonstrating evidence of potential illegal conduct (Zagaris 2002). Beyond the lack of evidence provided by the US government at the time, Swedish police also declared in November 2001 that they "were not suspected of any crime under national law" (Cramér 2003: 91). Negotiations at the Security Council continued, leading to the creation of a de-listing process that was announced by the Sanctions Committee in August 2002. Two of the three Swedish citizens were de-listed soon after under the new process (Cramér 2003: 94–5). Additionally, the Security Council modified its financial sanctions regime to address the humanitarian concern that the sanctions left individuals without the basic means to live. In December 2002 Resolution 1452 introduced a list of humanitarian exemptions when freezing the personal financial assets of named individuals. A short review of two influential European court cases is helpful to better understand the pressure behind the changes to introduce transparency and the right to challenge the targeted sanctions listing process at the Security Council.

Full Court Press against UN sanctions

One of the organizations added to the 1267 Consolidated Sanctions List at the request of the US in November 2001 was al Barakaat. At that time it was one of the largest firms in Somalia, providing money transfer and mobile phone services for the country. It was also a major conduit of remittances from the Somali diaspora in the US, Canada and European countries, back to their families in Somalia (Kaufman 2001). The al Barakaat International Foundation in Sweden was one of its affiliated companies. It was in the context of a money transfer company that the US government accused al Barakaat of being associated with Osama bin Laden and serving as "the quartermasters of terror", according to the US Treasury Secretary (Roth, Greenburg & Wille 2004: 80). Again, little demonstrable evidence was required for placement on the US sanctions list; as described in the *Monograph on Terrorist Financing*, government officials "relied on a derivative designation theory, in which no direct proof of culpability was needed" (Roth, Greenburg & Wille 2004: 79). The following year the US government removed the individuals associated with al Barakaat from its domestic list of "designated entities" (Roth, Greenburg & Wille 2004: 86). While some employees and customers of al Barakaat in the US were convicted of AML and welfare fraud charges, no one actually was charged with financing terrorism (Roth, Greenburg & Wille 2004: 86). Simultaneously, however, the company, its affiliates and many of its staff were placed on the sanctions list maintained by the 1267 Committee. Efforts to have them removed from the UN list when they were removed from the US sanctions list were actively resisted by US diplomats. "The State Department sent demarches to all Security Council member nations, urging 'in the strongest terms' that they oppose Swedish effort" to remove all names associated with al Barakaat from the list (Roth, Greenburg & Wille 2004: 85). Moreover, many of these individuals and affiliates of al Barakaat remained on the UN sanctions list in 2009 despite the point made in the *Monograph on Terrorist Financing* that there was no evidence supporting the accusations (Roth, Greenburg & Wille 2004: 85–6). The US Treasury continued to maintain publicly that "Barakaat organizations were part of a financial conglomerate operating in 40 countries around the world that facilitated the financing and operations of al Qaida and other terrorist organizations".

In September 2008 the European Court of Justice overturned the September 2006 Court of First Instance Judgement in the case of the al Barakaat International Foundation and Yassin Abdullah Kadi. When the asset freeze of al Barakaat and associated individuals was directed by the UN Security Council in 2001, action in the EU was coordinated using a European Commission regulation. This regulation transposed the 1267 Committee sanctions list into an EU sanctions list. The European Court of Justice ruled that the actions taken by the European Commission regulation had infringed individual fundamental rights and, as a result, it annulled the action to freeze their assets. Even though the Court agreed that the action to freeze financial assets might be justified, the EU had failed to inform either the al Barakaat International Foundation or Kadi at any time concerning the reasons used to justify their presence on the sanctions list. Consequently it was the opinion of the Court that they had been denied their right to legal recourse (European Court of Justice 2008). In November 2008, the European Commission reiterated that financial sanctions against both al Barakaat and Kadi were necessary and therefore they would be maintained. In the Regulation, (EC) No 1190/2008, published by the Commission it declared that "the listing of Al Barakaat International Foundation is justified for reasons of its association with the Al-Qaida network" (European Commission 2008: 25). This claim would suggest that the European Commission possessed intelligence information not available to the authors of the *Monograph on Terrorist Financing* when they stated there was no connection between al Barakaat and al Qaida, Osama bin Laden or terrorist financing (Roth, Greenburg & Wille 2004: 85–6). All the same, there has been no public revelation of evidence connecting al Barakaat to al Qaida.

As reported in a subsequent court case, the European Commission had informed Yassin Abdullah Kadi after it reimposed financial sanctions against him that it had examined his reply to their letter of October 2008:

> The Commission stated, in particular, that, in providing him with the summary of reasons provided by the UN Sanctions Committee and inviting him to comment on those reasons, it had complied with the

judgment of the Court of Justice in Kadi and that that judgment did not require it to disclose the further evidence which he had requested.
(General Court of the European Union 2010: n.p.)

As one may expect, this limited response by the European Commission to comply with the bare letter of the law was not well-received by the Court, noting in this press release that "it is evident from the arguments and explanations advanced by the Commission that Mr Kadi's rights of defence have been 'observed' only in the most formal and superficial sense" (General Court of the European Union 2010: n.p.). After iterating several other problems with the actions of the European Commission, the General Court of the European Union (formerly the Court of First Instance) decided in Mr Kadi's favour in September 2010 and annulled the regulation "in so far as it concerns Mr Kadi" (General Court of the European Union 2010: n.p.). Yassin Abdullah Kadi was a Saudi businessman that also had firms based in Switzerland as well as the EU and elsewhere. In the case he filed in Switzerland the judgement of the Swiss courts was similar, declaring that the prosecutor had failed to provide sufficient evidence (in open court) to justify the sanctions. It was the position of the Swiss government, however, that as long as he was on the UN Security Council's sanctions list, his assets in Switzerland would remain frozen (Whitlock 2008).

One aspect to appreciate when considering these court cases is the context of the legal arena(s) in which they exist. The individual named in the Security Council sanctions list at the request of a state had no mechanism as an individual to contest that action at the UN prior to the introduction of a "Focal Point for De-Listing" in 2006 (Gehring & Dörfler 2013: 579). This role of a focal point for de-listing was formalized with the establishment of the Office of the Ombudsperson in 2009 (see also Prost 2018). I have described this context elsewhere as a situation with "the participation of actors without a presence" (Vlcek 2009: 279). The named individual has no voice or presence within the conduct among states on the multilateral stage of the UN Security Council. They are, in essence, a disembodied presence attached to the name (and supporting documentation) inscribed on the request submitted for their addition to the sanctions list. Adding this role of Ombudsperson to the structure of targeted sanctions at the Security Council offered individuals with an avenue to directly challenge the decision to place them on the sanctions list. The path towards a successful de-listing remains, however, constrained. It relies on the cooperation of the state responsible for the listing to release its evidence, which can be difficult to achieve when it involves intelligence data that is considered "classified" (Minnella 2019: 48–9).

These two court cases in Europe may have gained the attention of many academics, but they are not unique.[2] The 2009 report of the Security Council's

Analytical Support and Sanctions Monitoring Team identified 13 legal challenges to the targeted sanctions world-wide; in addition to those in the EU, there was litigation at the European Court of Human Rights, and in Pakistan, the UK and the US (Analytical Support and Sanctions Monitoring Team 2009: 32–4). Even after a decade of operation, the work of the Office of the Ombudsperson had not completely replaced national litigation against inclusion on the sanctions list.[3] The report of the Analytical Support and Sanctions Monitoring Team in 2021 continues to list three court cases ongoing in Pakistan (Analytical Support and Sanctions Monitoring Team 2021a: 23). Nonetheless, it has helped to address the concern that litigation against targeted sanctions would undermine the authority of the UN Security Council to act against terrorism. And to some extent, the initial lack of due process did reduce the willingness of a number of states to support the Security Council agenda (Biersteker, Eckert & Romaniuk 2008: 247).

In large part, the initial approach of the UN Security Council reflected the desires of the permanent members, and especially the US as the target of the September 2001 terrorist attacks (Gehring, Dorsch & Dörfler 2019: 125–8).[4] The political dimension of sanctions, listing the accused without provisions for rebuttal and correction, may be conceived as an "ends justifies the means" approach to counterterrorism at the beginning of the century. Measures against terrorist financing were the first move taken against al Qaida in September 2001, but later actions by the US, such as their programme of extraordinary rendition and the apparent acceptance of torture ("to find the ticking bomb"), equally serve as elements of an "ends justifies the means" counterterrorism strategy. At the same time, not all participants in the creation of the international CFT regime were confident of its effectiveness in stopping terrorism. Taylor, for example, felt that US measures against terrorist financing were "helped" by Resolution 1373 (2001), "But based on past experience with compliance of UN Resolutions, I knew our direct contact with other finance ministries would be essential" (Taylor 2007: 12). The implication of this statement is that direct contact by US government officials had more impact on foreign government actions than did an obligation to comply with the Security Council. The challenge of compliance with the international CFT regime is explored further in Chapter 5.

Continuing evolution of targeted sanctions for CFT

Another adjustment responding to the criticism over the lack of due process in the work of the Sanctions Committee was made with Resolution 1822 (2008). It consolidated the preceding Resolutions and provided for the continuation of existing financial sanctions against those listed. Additionally, the Resolution addressed the concern over transparency of the processes followed by the 1267

Sanctions Committee when it decided to impose sanctions. The changes included releasing public data on the Committee's website to explain why a person or group was listed and subjected to sanctions.[5] The Resolution also imposed duties on states that were involved with the process or home to a listed person or group. States need to notify those listed of that action and provide them with a copy of the public data, and also to notify them when they are removed from the sanctions list. Finally it directed that the sanctions list be reviewed periodically to ensure accuracy of the data, including information regarding the incarceration or death of anyone on the sanctions list.

Where many Security Council Resolutions concerned with terrorist financing involve targeted sanctions, Resolution 1617 (2005) makes the first explicit reference to the FATF and its Forty Recommendations. The Resolution "Strongly urges all Member States to implement the comprehensive, international standards embodied in the Financial Action Task Force's (FATF) Forty Recommendations on Money Laundering and the FATF Nine Special Recommendations on Terrorist Financing" (¶7). As with the preceding Resolutions it was introduced under Chapter VII, and therefore, with this sentence urging all member states to comply with the FATF Forty Recommendations, Security Council Resolution 1617 becomes the foundation for an international regime against terrorist finance operating through the activity of the FATF.

This directive to implement and enforce the Forty Recommendations was reinforced in subsequent Security Council Resolutions. Islamic State was incorporated into the UN targeted sanctions regime with Security Council Resolution 2253 (2015). The Resolution further highlighted FATF Recommendation 6, which directs states to comply with the Security Council sanctions regime (¶16), and "welcomes" the FATF reports released in 2015 on the financing of IS and "Emerging Terrorist Financing Risks" (¶17). Two years later Resolution 2368 (2017) substantially repeated the text of these paragraphs. The work of the Counterterrorism Committee Executive Directorate (CTED) was the focus of Resolution 2395 (2017), and paragraph 25 reiterated the work of the FATF while "encouraging" the CTED to cooperate closely with it. In Resolution 2462 (2019) the Security Council moved beyond simply reminding states that they are "strongly urged" to implement the Forty Recommendations (¶4). It also specifies that their actions against terrorism (including terrorist financing) must be compliant with international humanitarian law (¶6), that they must establish a financial intelligence unit (¶15; see also FATF Recommendation 28), and also that they must ensure that all financial transactions are transparent and traceable (¶20; see also the interpretive note for FATF Recommendation 16).

The circular nature of these instruments, the UN Security Council Resolutions with the FATF Forty Recommendations, should be clear.[6] They direct states to implement and enforce the Forty Recommendations. In turn, one of these

Recommendations (#6) directs the implementation of the Security Council Resolutions imposing targeted sanctions, Resolutions that are now also directing the implementation of the Forty Recommendations. And recall that the first Special Recommendation on terrorist financing directed states to ratify and implement the Convention for the Suppression of the Financing of Terrorism (1999). With the ratification of the treaty by most UN member states, that Recommendation was no longer necessary when the Forty Recommendations were revised in 2012. In this way, the "de facto international standard" produced by the FATF (a limited membership club) has become the foundation for an international regime to combat the financing of terrorism within the commitments of UN member states under Chapter VII of the UN Charter (Prost 2018: 920).

The political dimension of targeted sanctions returned to the forefront in June 2011 when the Security Council found that it needed to adjust the structure of the 1267 Sanctions Committee to support negotiations with the Taliban (Minnella 2019: 34). Two new Resolutions broke the explicit connection that had existed between the Taliban and al Qaida before then. Sanctions against the Taliban were now managed under Resolution 1988 (2011), with its own targeted sanctions list to support the efforts at conflict resolution and reconstruction in Afghanistan. With a separate sanctions Resolution, suspending or cancelling it could be offered as part of the negotiations with the Taliban to end the conflict in Afghanistan. Responsibility for maintaining the targeted sanctions list for al Qaida and its associates was placed in Resolution 1989 (2011). The Security Council highlighted its concerns over the use of kidnapping for ransom as a source of terrorist financing with Resolution 2133 (2014). In particular, the Resolution encouraged inter-state cooperation against the use of ransom payments for terrorist financing and requested that the CTC arrange a special meeting to evaluate measures to prevent the use of kidnapping for this purpose.

IS forced further changes to the counterterrorism approach of the Security Council, starting with Resolution 2170 (2014), when IS, along with the Al Nusrah Front, were named as groups associated with al Qaida. The Resolution placed them under the obligations established by Resolution 1373 (2001) and the prevention of terrorist financing, with six individuals added to the sanctions list. Moreover, Resolution 2170 (2014) noted the control of oilfields as an additional source of income for IS, Al Nusrah Front and others associated with al Qaida. Subsequently, with Resolution 2253 (2015), the Security Council reorganized the Sanctions Committee to incorporate IS. The "1267/1989 Al-Qaida Sanctions Committee" was reconstituted as the "1267/1989/2253 ISIL (Da'esh) and Al-Qaida Sanctions Committee" by Security Council Resolution 2253 in 2015. In addition to the targeted sanctions for anyone supporting IS, the Security Council also attempted to address the growth of extremist material on the internet and social media. IS and its financing dimension are covered further in Chapter 7.

Consistent with the fact that any economic transaction may be used to support terrorist financing, the Security Council has addressed the linkages between terrorism and organized crime, illegal goods trafficking and human trafficking. In 2016 the Security Council encouraged member states "to take decisive and immediate action" against human trafficking in Resolution 2331 (2016), particularly when it involved a conflict zone and the movement of refugees. This Resolution specifically noted the actions of IS and other terrorist groups in using human trafficking as a source of income (¶11). The Security Council followed Resolution 2331 (2016) in 2017 with Resolution 2388. It reiterated and reinforced the earlier call to act against human trafficking, and requested reports on the role of human trafficking in support of terrorist groups and terrorist financing. This concern, along with the linkage between organized crime and terrorist groups, was further raised in Resolution 2482 (2019), with a call to member states to strengthen their enforcement of the UN Convention against Transnational Organized Crime (2000) and the UN Convention against Corruption (2003), along with the UN Convention for the Suppression of the Financing of Terrorism. One report produced in response to these Resolutions considered the interplay of terrorist financing and human trafficking, kidnapping for ransom, modern slavery, and organ removal and sale (Counter-Terrorism Committee Executive Directorate 2019).

Organizing the UN to counter terrorism

The structures of the UN for counterterrorism have evolved over the past two decades to address changes in strategy and approach over this time. From the initial actions of the Security Council in the late twentieth century, the scope and application of targeted sanctions grew and the CTC was established, with several offices to support it (several of which have already been mentioned). In the beginning there was the 1267 Committee, which maintained the list of those placed under targeted sanctions as directed by Resolution 1267. It is the case that the responsibility of the Committee grew beyond those named in Resolution 1267 to include al Qaida and IS, along with those individuals and groups identified as associated with them. The Committee remains one of the subsidiary bodies formed within the Security Council responsible for monitoring the participation of the UN member states in the sanctions regime first created by Resolution 1267, as well as being responsible for maintaining the sanctions list itself.

Although the sanctions list was first established by Resolution 1267, the CTC was created by Resolution 1373 in September 2001. It is responsible for monitoring the implementation of the measures directed by the Resolution, including reports to be submitted by countries that outline the progress they have made in implementing the specified measures against terrorism. The membership of the CTC is identical to the Security Council and it is assisted by the CTED. The CTED was established in 2004 by Security Council Resolution 1535 (2004) in order to strengthen and coordinate the process of monitoring the implementation of Resolution 1373 (2001). It helps by carrying out the policy decisions of the Committee, conducting expert assessments of each UN member state and by facilitating counterterrorism technical assistance missions. In 2019 the scope of its responsibility was extended with Resolution 2462 (2019), which asked it to conduct "targeted and focused follow-up visits as complements to its comprehensive assessments". The objective was to improve CTED assessments beyond the data submitted by member states and to identify any need for a technical assistance mission or for capacity building.

The Analytical Support and Sanctions Monitoring Team was created in 2004 by Resolution 1526 to assess the effectiveness of the sanctions process. Its reports provide an analysis on the effectiveness of the sanctions list and the implementation of those sanctions, including the freezing of assets, the ban on travel and the arms embargo. What becomes apparent from their reports over time is a problem with getting states to submit the reports required by Resolution 1373. The problem has been called "reporting fatigue" because not only is the UN Security Council asking for this information, a number of other international organizations are requesting the same, or very similar, information too, including the FATF, the local FSRB, the International Monetary Fund (IMF), the World Bank, and even academics conducting research on the subject of terrorist finance. For small and developing economies that do not feel threatened by transnational terrorism, the time and money necessary to deal with these information requests reduces their ability to deal with other issues that are of greater importance for their citizens. One result is that some states cut and paste from one report into a new document when responding to the latest request for updated information. Another is that countries simply stop submitting reports.

As developed through this chapter it should be clear that the Security Council has been the central location for action against terrorist financing at the UN. By issuing the relevant Resolutions under Chapter VII of the UN charter it has obligated the member states to take the actions directed in those Resolutions (Prost 2018: 912). The process of imposing targeted sanctions was criticized, as discussed previously, for the failure to recognize human rights in their design, and specifically for the absence of due process procedures in the early years. Additionally, international law scholars questioned whether the early actions of the Security Council meant it operated as a "global legislator" when making Resolutions obligatory under Chapter VII (Powell 2018: 885; Rosand 2005). These Resolutions do more than just obligate states to implement and enforce sanctions against terrorist financing. This obligation extends to explicitly directing changes to domestic law, thus effectively legislating for the UN member states (de Londras 2019: 208–12). Moreover, the actions of the permanent five members of the Security Council (China, France, Russia, the UK and the US) to exercise control over the counterterrorism mandate were called "imperial" and "neocolonial" by some observers (Minnella 2019: 35; see also, de Londras 2019: 236–7). This criticism, and the resistance of a number of states against continued cooperation with the approach of the Security Council, led not only to changes in Security Council practice but also to increased refinement of a counterterrorism agenda by the Secretary-General and the General Assembly of the UN.

One initial step was the establishment of the Counter-Terrorism Implementation Task Force in 2005. It was created by the Secretary-General "to bring together key actors in the United Nations system and its partners dealing with counter-terrorism issues" (United Nations General Assembly 2006: ¶3). This group then crafted a strategy and Recommendations to organize the disparate counterterrorism initiatives undertaken across the UN system (beyond the Security Council), while maintaining human rights as a central component of that strategy. The General Assembly accepted this strategy report and adopted its Recommendations as the "United Nations Global Counter-Terrorism Strategy" in 2006.[7] Section II of the annex to this General Assembly Resolution encourages states to implement the FATF Forty Recommendations in paragraph 10. Agreeing to a strategy, however, does not assure that all participating agencies, and the member states they support, will consistently cooperate on the various aspects of the counterterrorism strategy (Schindler 2020: 172–3). In order to improve the coordination of UN counterterrorism activities, the UN Office of Counter-Terrorism was established in 2017.[8]

Throughout the development of the counterterrorism structure of the UN by the Secretary-General and the General Assembly, addressing the financing of terrorism has been just one element of its purpose. The UN Office of Counter-Terrorism coordinates a broad-based strategy for tackling terrorism and its root causes as much as it is a strategy for preventing acts of terrorism. Consequently, the main locus for combatting terrorist financing within the UN remains under the scope (and control) of the Security Council. This circumstance remains problematic because the Security Council Resolutions serve to mandate obligations on states that may be beyond the capacity of the states to implement, regardless of the desires of the government. And the extent to which human rights are still not recognized and included within more recent Resolutions continues to be identified (de Londras 2019: 215–18). Capacity, however, remains a critical limitation for the implementation and enforcement of AML/CFT for many countries. In addition to requiring technical assistance and external funding, this limiting factor also forced a recognition among FATF member states that there are significant differences among national financial systems, for example the widespread operation of *hawala* and other informal financial practices. The FATF, in turn, refined its guidance with the introduction of a risk-based approach to address some of these differences, as explored in the next chapter.

5

MAKING CFT GLOBAL

Making the regime to counter terrorist financing global is more than simply expecting UN members to comply with the Resolutions of the Security Council. Yet that is the expectation of the Security Council, that all states are committed to take these actions because they are issued under Chapter VII of the UN Charter. The periodic reports of the Analytical Support and Sanctions Monitoring Team on compliance for the resolutions that impose targeted sanctions to prevent terrorist financing, however, reveal that is not the case. Beyond reporting data on accounts and assets frozen, states are expected to maintain travel bans, arms embargos and all other forms of targeted sanctions. For several states the cost of compliance, in the context of local conditions and with limited national resources, is simply too much. Financial and technical support is available but not as a permanent and ongoing subsidy to cover the continuing cost of compliance. The result is differing levels of implementation and enforcement among the member states of the UN, reflecting their level of concern for transnational terrorism and the local capacity to establish and enforce the CFT regime. As seen later in the chapter, if the FATF feels that a country's effort to act against money laundering and terrorist financing is insufficient, it will impose its measures intended to encourage the government to correct the deficiencies.

Even in countries with extensive formal financial systems and high levels of financial inclusion, the introduction of CFT measures at the beginning of the twenty-first century was not straightforward. An official from the UK's Financial Services Authority related one example of the problems created by them in a conference speech in 2004: An "Oxford College [was] required to produce its 15th century charter, complete with seal to open a new account" (Robinson 2004: n.p.). The issue highlighted by this anecdote is the extent to which bank employees might require documentation to prove identity to satisfy the customer due diligence (CDD) requirement (also known as the "know your customer" obligation). The requirement is to prove one's legal identity so that the bank can avoid providing services to an individual or business that is the subject of targeted sanctions.

For this particular Oxford college, its identity as a recognized entity was based on a historical Royal Charter where a modern company would provide proof of its corporate registration. Individuals similarly demonstrate proof of their identity using a government-issued document along with a document (often a utility bill) showing their residential address. Many residents of a developed economy have no problem satisfying these CDD requirements, but that is not the case in other economies. Individuals unable to prove identity to comply with this CDD obligation are excluded from the formal financial system as a result, which has developmental consequences.

There are two levels explored in the following five sections on the experience of the global CFT regime. First there is the state level of implementation: compliance and enforcement as overseen by the FATF and its regional partners. And then there is the experience of the ordinary citizen in opening a financial account and transferring money across borders (particularly migrant remittances).[1] This individual or everyday level of experience is introduced in the next section. The second section expands the discussion to include the risk-based approach introduced by the FATF as a means for mitigating the impact of the CDD obligation as a barrier to financial inclusion. Financial institutions attempt to comply with their role in the global CFT regime while also operating as a profitable financial business. One unintended consequence of the impact of CFT on these private actors is known as derisking, which is explored in the third section. The operation of non-profit organizations in conflict zones has become challenging because of derisking practices and CDD obligations. These issues, combined with the misuse of charities for terrorist financing, are covered in the fourth section. The final section of the chapter is focused on the state level, and the measures employed by the FATF and its member states to make the CFT regime global.

Informal economies and migrant remittances

The global CFT regime is built on two fundamental features: that the country has a financial system composed of registered, regulated financial firms; and that all individual people and companies possess government-approved identity documentation. The first feature ensures the financial system can monitor and track all economic transactions to identify potential terrorist financing (and money laundering). And the second feature is necessary to know and record who is involved in those financial transactions as well as to prevent known terrorist financiers from accessing the financial system of that country. The expectation that each country possesses these two features means that the CFT regime has gaps where the expectation has not been fully met. These gaps occur where the territory has financial transactions occurring outside of a formal financial system using unregistered, unregulated individuals and firms. It was a concern over such gaps that drove the requirement to register everyone involved in the money service business, as discussed in Chapter 3. Ensuring that everyone possesses a government-approved identity document is also a challenge, and is discussed in more detail in the next section.

Central to informal economies are the money service and informal value transfer businesses (such as *hawala*) that were introduced in Chapter 3. Again, part of the concern surrounding their use by terrorist groups was due to an unfamiliarity with these financial practices along with a perception that they do not keep transaction records. Even for those small MSBs and *hawaladars* that use a bank or other financial firm to transfer money, the recorded identity information will be for the MSB/*hawaladar* and not for the originator or final recipient of the money. It is the identity details for the originator and recipient that are desired and necessary to satisfy CFT requirements. Nonetheless, the IVTS continues to exist and function because it satisfies a need, whether for the quick, cheap and fast transfer of money or because it works with customers unable to open a traditional bank account. To understand the demand for IVTSs, it helps to understand the environment in which they operate, commonly known as the "informal" economy.

The concept of the informal economy is attributed to the staff of the Institute of Development Studies, University of Nairobi, by the authors of a 1972 report on labour and employment in Kenya for the International Labour Organization (ILO) (Bangasser 2000: 10). In the context of labour and employment, for the ILO the informal economy consists of either informal employment or working for an informal employer. The distinction is that an informal employer is one that is not registered with the government, while informal employment is cash-in-hand, be it self-employed, working for a family member or working "off-the-books" for a registered (formal) business (ILO 2012: 27). An informal economy consisting of legal activities performed by unregistered businesses that are not paying taxes (and other regulatory gaps) is often conflated with the illegal or underground economy consisting of illegal activities. The latter activities are those explicitly against local laws, frequently including recreational drugs and prostitution. Efforts to measure the size of any country's informal economy are problematic because these economic activities are clandestine and neither reported nor formally measured.[2] While the size of the informal economy in some countries may be as high as 64.9 per cent of the total national economy (Georgia), even a small informal economy (Switzerland: 7.2 per cent) may conceal informal financial activity, including terrorist financing (Medina & Schneider 2018: 23).

The size of the informal economy offers a sense of the relative demand for informal financial services because it also provides a sense of the level of financial inclusion. Financial inclusion is understood as affordable access to a variety of financial services, including savings and credit. It also includes access for under-served groups, those with low or intermittent incomes or the undocumented. The lack of documentation is one barrier to financial inclusion because of the registered financial institution's CDD obligation for AML/CFT compliance. These same financial institutions also desire to be profitable businesses, which encourages them to avoid low-income customers that will be unprofitable. Access to an account is further limited by the availability of a bank branch or ATM, which are mostly located in urban areas. The World Bank reported that in 2017 there were 1.7 billion adults globally without a financial account (at a bank or mobile money company). It emphasized that "[b]ecause account owner-ship is nearly universal in high-income economies, virtually all unbanked adults live in developing economies" (Demirgüç-Kunt *et al.* 2018: 35). The attention on financial inclusion, by the World Bank, development agencies and, ultim-ately, the FATF, is because access to financial services has been demonstrated to improve economic development. Access provides people with a safer way to save money than placing it in a jar under the bed, and savings, in turn, offer the means to invest in health care, education and home businesses (Demirgüç-Kunt *et al.* 2018: 1).

As discussed in Chapter 3, the recognition of the extent of informal methods used to transfer money in the global economy was accompanied by the identifi-cation of migrant remittances as a major user of these financial services. Global aggregate figures for migrant remittances are substantial (an estimated $702 billion in 2020), yet these flows are uneven and variable among countries (Ratha *et al.* 2021: 3). Some states are large receiving destinations by quantity (the top three being India, $83 billion; China, $60 billion; and Mexico, $43 billion). However, when remittance flows are considered as a percentage of national gross domestic product (GDP) a different ordering of countries is produced (the top three being Tonga, 38 per cent; Lebanon, 33 per cent; and Kyrgyz Republic, 29 per cent) (Ratha *et al.* 2021: 6). The point, once again, is that these figures represent many small transfers, money sent home by migrant labour that is very price-conscious for the cost of an individual transfer. The cost of making a transfer using one of the formal routes for which data is collected and reported ranges from 4.9 per cent in South Asia to 8.2 per cent in Sub-Saharan Africa. The global average in the fourth quarter of 2020 was 6.5 per cent, and all of these figures remain above the Sustainable Development Goal (SDG) target of 3 per cent by 2030 (Ratha *et al.* 2021: 16–18). The authors of this report are aware of the impact that AML/CFT requirements have on the remittance transfer sector. They refer to the problems facing the individuals sending remittances (lack of required identity documents) as well as describing these regulations in combin-ation with bank derisking practices as "onerous for new market entrants using new technologies" (Ratha *et al.* 2021: 18). These new technologies, including mobile money, are covered in Chapter 6.

This discussion of migrant remittances is not intended to suggest that only migrant labourers sending money home face these problems with access to the formal financial system. A very similar experience awaits anyone unable to present an acceptable identity document and proof of residence. Citizens without a government-approved document are equally prevented from access, along with anyone living in an informal community (e.g. *barrio, favela* or other form of shanty town), even when they have acceptable identification documents. This informal economic environment combined with the barriers to access the formal financial sector serve to sustain the demand for informal financial services. Moreover, the cost of transferring remittances via a registered, formal-sector financial firm encourages the continued use of IVTSs even if the individual has the necessary documentation because of the lower cost. The continued operation of IVTSs is seen as providing terrorists and terrorist groups a way to avoid the CFT regime. Consequently, the FATF and others have sought to reduce the barriers to access and minimize the incentives for using an IVTS. The next section discusses the adjustments introduced by the FATF to address the situation.

RBA, CDD and financial inclusion

The FATF secretariat and member states came to recognize the challenges facing some national financial systems of implementing the Forty Recommendations. In response, it developed a method for scaling the requirements to reflect the level of relative risk posed by any individual customer. This risk-based approach (RBA) was established by a working group composed of representatives from the banking and securities industries, and the first document describing it was the "Guidance on the Risk-Based Approach to Combating Money Laundering and Terrorist Finance: High Level Principles and Procedures" in 2007. The guidance document set the foundations for the scope and parameters of a methodology to implement the Forty Recommendations. In particular it "implies the adoption of a risk management process for" AML/CFT implementation and enforcement. One section focused on the implementation approach for government agencies and a second section provided implementation guidance for the financial sector. The RBA involves a process of evaluating the nature and level of risk for money laundering and terrorist financing, by the government for the whole country and by financial institutions for their current and potential customers. It remains important to maintain the capacity to identify and report potential money laundering following the introduction of RBA-compliant adjustments to AML/CFT policies. As the guidance document points out, however, we can expect that people will continue to find ways to move their illicit assets through the banking system. The FATF emphasis on illicit money is due to the fact that the nature of terrorist financing methods makes it more difficult to assess the risks. This distinction, however, may not be reflected in the introduction of the RBA to national AML/CFT regulations.

The FATF expanded the RBA with a series of further guidance documents looking at specific business sectors, including money/value transfer businesses, mobile money and virtual assets (popularly known as cryptocurrencies). For the MSBs, the guidance centred not only on the risks associated with the sender but also the risks associated with the destination of the money. Government guidance concerned the design of a regulatory framework for evaluating the methods employed by the MSB for mitigating risk as well as determining the nature of the risk for money laundering or terrorist financing in the country. The MSBs need to be aware of the risks associated with potential customers and the risks attributed to destination countries. The latter risks are determined by reference to the country's presence on an FATF or UN list. Additionally, MSB firms that use agents and subagents with direct customer contact must also assess the risks posed by their agents/subagents as potential facilitators of money laundering or terrorist financing. Registered MSBs and IVTSs are obligated to conduct CDD on those sending money and report suspicious transactions to national authorities. An additional level of guidance involves the banks that provide financial services to MSBs and IVTSs, and implementing an RBA in these business relationships. The central element of FATF guidance regarding MSBs remains the same, that registration is essential to ensure CDD compliance and the reporting of suspicious activity. At the same time, this emphasis excludes migrant labour without the means to satisfy the CDD requirement, preventing them from using these services to send remittances and forcing them to use unregistered (underground) services that continue to operate outside of the enforcement regime.

The guidance for mobile money was grouped with prepaid cards and internet-based payment systems under the heading of "new payment products and services" when it was released in 2013. The concern is that these new payment methods could be misused for money laundering or terrorist financing because they may operate in ways that are not covered by the Forty Recommendations. And each of them does offer ways to avoid the regulatory oversight expected by the FATF, for example, through anonymous access or usage. As discussed in more detail in Chapter 6, mobile money is different from using a mobile phone to access a retail bank account. A mobile money account can be with the mobile phone service provider connected to the mobile phone number and money can be transferred to anyone who also has an account with the mobile money company. Where opening and maintaining a bank account involves providing documentation to meet the bank's CDD obligation, that may not be the case with the mobile money company, which opens up a gap for money laundering or terrorist financing. Several methods have been implemented by mobile money companies to reduce the risk of misuse, including face-to-face account opening with an employee/agent of the mobile money service provider and setting limits on the amount of money that can be stored in an account, along with limits on the amount that can be withdrawn from it in a transaction/day.

Many of the same concerns about the risk for money laundering or terrorist financing seen in MSBs and mobile money are present in virtual money/assets. In 2019 the FATF updated its 2015 guidance document for applying an RBA to virtual currencies, incorporating changes introduced to the Forty Recommendations in 2018 to "explicitly clarify that they apply to financial activities involving virtual assets". The FATF titled this guidance document, "Guidance for a Risk-based Approach: Virtual Assets and Virtual Asset Service Providers", and foremost among the concerns identified is anonymity. Anonymity has been a cornerstone of virtual currencies and a design feature for many of them from the start. Consequently, virtual currencies and other virtual financial assets are viewed by regulators as a danger to the financial system because of the potential for criminal misuse. The FATF guidance and approach for dealing with virtual currencies is changing to keep up with the evolution of the technology and its usage. The issue continues to be with CDD and AML/CFT compliance, which remains in opposition to the presence of anonymity in many virtual currencies. Operationally, the FATF broadly defines the virtual asset as the "digital representation of value that can be digitally traded, or transferred, and can be used for payment or investment purposes". It further specifies that the virtual asset is not a "digital representation" for any financial asset already covered by the Forty Recommendations, such as fiat currencies and precious metals. The application of the RBA to virtual currencies is substantially identical to MSBs and mobile money services. In addition to implementing CDD and maintaining records of customer transactions, the virtual asset service providers are expected to report suspicious transactions and monitor for transactions involving high-risk destination countries.

The centrality of anonymity to virtual assets highlights the emphasis placed on CDD throughout the AML/CFT regime as a pivotal component to identify and prevent access to those individuals involved in money laundering and terrorist financing. The first step in the CDD process at a financial institution is to establish the identity of the prospective customer using government-approved documents, including those issued by recognized non-governmental organizations, such as utility companies, displaying a residential address. Identity documents start with accurately reporting data on a person from birth and maintaining the record in a secure manner to produce a government identification document. In some

countries reporting and maintaining accurate data on citizens has been difficult, often relying on incomplete paper-based records. Moreover, the reliability
of verifying the residential address can be challenging, when in Sub-Saharan
Africa, for example, many countries do not have a "centralised address repository against which the proof of address can be verified" (Symington, Thom &
van der Linden 2020: 21). India, on the other hand, has undertaken a national
biometric data collection programme to overcome the lack of accurate data on
its citizens. The Aadhaar programme provides a mechanism to verify identity by
linking the Aadhaar number to the individual's biometric profile data, which is
then available electronically to be checked by public service and welfare offices.
The resulting database can help to reduce fraud in welfare systems in addition
to satisfying the CDD obligation, so increasing financial inclusion (Amicelle &
Jacobsen 2016: 95–7).[3] It is a time-consuming and expensive process to produce
a biometric database of the national population, but it is under consideration by
other countries with similar objectives (Martin 2021).

The benefits of financial inclusion for economic development, for the individual and for society at large, are recognized. The FATF introduced yet another
benefit from its perspective and focus on AML/CFT: that financial inclusion
promotes AML/CFT compliance and enforcement because financial exclusion
effectively counters compliance activity. The operation of an informal economy
with widespread use of cash for economic transactions is framed by the FATF
as a threat not only to the AML/CFT regime of the country but also to the
integrity of its banking system. Merging this concern with the developmental
benefits of financial inclusion situates the FATF as a supporter of financial
inclusion because the large, cash-based informal economy could serve as a
shelter for money laundering and terrorist financing. This perspective was
echoed at that time by a World Bank study because it was consistent with a
concern for the role of "ill-gotten money" in the economies under analysis.
This effort to study the circulation of illicit money in Malawi and Namibia
led the authors to conclude that "financial inclusion and AML are comple-
mentary goals in both Malawi and Namibia, because the widespread use of
cash reduces the effectiveness of the AML system" (Yikona *et al.* 2011: 87).
The 2017 update to the FATF report on AML/CFT and financial inclusion
re-emphasized its concerns and added that financial inclusion "improved consumer protection against fraud, financial abuse and exploitation". The quotable
conclusion offered was that "Financial inclusion and financial integrity are thus
mutually reinforcing". This conclusion has not, however, been found by empirical research in Sub-Saharan Africa, where customer choice regarding the use
of informal financial services is shaped by concerns over government surveillance (the AML/CFT regime) operating within formal financial services (de
Koker & Jentzsch 2013).

The RBA methodology is centred on the formal banking system, even where the CDD requirements are reduced to facilitate access to special, low-risk bank accounts. The use of cash in the informal economy means that it functions beyond the reach of the AML/CFT structure implemented within the formal banking sector. As a result, cash itself becomes treated as the adversary for governments and the FATF because it facilitates and conceals money laundering and terrorist financing. The argument for eliminating cash from the economy (whatever the justification) is neither novel nor very likely to succeed in the near future (for one example of this argument, see Rogoff 2016). To replace cash with its digital equivalent requires more than the introduction of reduced CDD requirements; it also requires access to the digital infrastructure and the electricity to power it all. These hurdles exist in the rural areas of large developed economies as much as they exist in countries with large informal economies. Mobile money (as discussed in Chapter 6) is widely seen as one remedy for achieving higher levels of financial inclusion, but infrastructure access for individuals and merchants also remains a hurdle to be overcome (Ahmad, Green & Jiang 2020). In the meantime, banks have implemented additional risk management approaches to reduce their risk of becoming implicated in either money laundering or terrorist financing. The result of these approaches has become known as "derisking", as explained in the next section.

Safe financial systems and derisking

The RBA looks at the risks involving financial services' customers and the implementation of the FATF Forty Recommendations. The guidance released for implementing the RBA addresses the processes to be employed when assessing the risks of any individual customer or business, and for the government it points to the processes for assessing the risks of the financial services firm. Looking, for example, at the guidance on implementing an RBA in the MSB sector, the authors of this guidance acknowledge the function performed by MSBs and IVTSs to support financial inclusion and migrant remittances. Further, the implementation of an RBA for the sector could promote financial inclusion and discourage the campaigns that are closing non-compliant service providers. The latter activity may be encouraging customers to use an unregistered, underground MSB/IVTS. The risk assessment performed by a registered and regulated MSB/IVTS involves determining the level of risk associated with several factors. These factors include the firm's customer base, the regions that it transmits money to, the regions it receives money from, the intermediation agents it uses to transfer and receive money and even the risk associated with the intended recipient. The RBA is an ongoing continuous process, as details about each factor, along with world circumstances, change the level of risk involved with that individual factor.

By stating that financial inclusion and financial integrity are "mutually reinforcing", the FATF is revisiting the claim that money laundering and terrorist financing are a threat to the financial system (Reuter & Truman 2004: 129–38). It is a claim that has also been made in World Bank publications, and critiqued by researchers for its lack of supporting empirical research (van Duyne, Harvey & Gelemerova 2018: 6–10). Further, it moves the onus for the integrity of the financial system from money laundering and terrorist financing onto the financial institutions themselves rather than with regulatory and law enforcement agencies. Ensuring that a financial firm is compliant with the AML/CFT regime and continuously updating the risk assessment of its customers, prospective customers and counter-parties requires a specialist staff. Increased compliance costs have been a significant marker of the shift and privatization of financial system integrity and security to financial firms. Studies commissioned by KPMG offered estimates for the cost of compliance based on survey responses collected from multinational banks. The respondents in 2004 indicated that compliance costs had increased 61 per cent over the preceding three years, and they expected the costs to increase a further 43 per cent in the subsequent three years (KPMG International 2004: 9). A decade later the survey reported that the cost of compliance had been regularly underestimated, with actual costs over the previous three years increasing, on average, by 53 per cent, when the expectation had been for only an average 40 per cent increase (KPMG International 2014: 7). A later study for the UK reported in 2018 that the financial sector staff involved in compliance numbered 11,500 and estimated that AML/CFT compliance cost the sector over £650 million a year (FCA 2018: 6).

The high cost of compliance has motivated financial firms to find cost-effective alternatives, which includes avoiding any business with a potentially risky customer. The FATF description of derisking is "the phenomenon of financial institutions terminating or restricting business relationships with clients or categories of clients to avoid, rather than manage, risk in line with the FATF's risk-based approach".[4] It seeks to deflect responsibility from the AML/CFT regime, and the FATF press release goes on to emphasize the multiple reasons behind any individual firm's business decision to withdraw from a market. The reasons listed are "concerns about profitability, prudential requirements, anxiety after the global financial crisis, and reputational risk". To some extent this assessment is valid, from the viewpoint of the FATF Secretariat sitting in Paris. For businesses in Africa, the Caribbean and elsewhere, their experience with derisking argues differently. In fact, one study from a think tank based in Cape Town, South Africa, using the FATF definition for the derisking phenomenon, identified the FATF as the global AML/CFT regulator and stated

"Thus, de-risking is a phenomenon that takes place in the context of AML-CFT" (Cooper *et al.* 2020: 8). Moreover, the phenomenon of derisking was recognized a decade earlier, even though the term itself was not used. In an assessment of the "Challenge to banks in implementing AML/CFT standards" the authors discussed the actions taken by banks. Framed as the results of a bank's cost/benefit analysis, the example provided was of banks in the US closing the accounts of MSBs and the concerns that it raised with banking regulators in early 2005 (Johnston & Carrington 2006: 58–9; citing Board of Govenors of the Federal Reserve System *et al.* 2005).

Derisking is essentially private market actors, on their own initiative, taking actions comparable to those directly mandated by the FATF. The FATF regularly updates a list of states that it has identified as having failed to properly implement and enforce AML/CFT guidance. These FATF actions were named "capital market sanctions" in one study of international soft law in global finance (Brummer 2012: 151–4). As of June 2021, for example, the FATF directed "all members and urge[d] all jurisdictions to apply enhanced due diligence, and in the most serious cases, countries are called upon to apply counter-measures to protect the international financial system" on all financial transactions with the Democratic People's Republic of Korea and Iran. The effect of this pronouncement is that the FATF has implemented international financial sanctions on these states in an effort to force a change in their domestic financial system governance.[5] The consequences for a financial institution that failed to implement "enhanced due diligence" on transactions with these two states could result in fines and penalties imposed by their home regulator and/or the US.[6] As a proactive measure against the potential for a jurisdiction to appear on the FATF's list in the future the international bank can choose to reduce the risk (and costs) of exposure by leaving the jurisdiction, closing its branches and correspondent accounts. A similar logic comes into play regarding a domestic regulator's potential future action against an individual, company or business sector, when the bank chooses to close the account(s) now as a proactive measure against the risk of future compliance enforcement action and penalties. Examples of derisking help to situate the context and impact, both at the local level and at the national/international level.

At the local level in the UK MSBs had an experience similar to those in the US when firms that sent remittances to Somalia found themselves without bank accounts. The last bank to serve these MSBs announced in early 2013 that it would be closing their accounts because of the potential for misuse for money laundering or terrorist financing. One concern was over the flow of remittances to Somalia when "large swaths of the rural hinterland remain controlled by al-Qaeda-linked al-Shabaab" (Flood 2013: n.p.). The logic that money going to family members in this area could directly or indirectly be transferred to (or taxed by) al-Shabaab meant that the MSB could be held responsible for facilitating terrorist financing. The affected companies responded to this suggestion by pointing out that closing their accounts prevented migrants from using a registered MSB and forced them to use an unregistered transfer agent. These "underground" transactions would be untracked and outside of the scope of the AML/CFT regime. One prominent case involved Barclays Bank's decision to close the UK account of Dahabshiil. This MSB challenged the closure of its account in court, leading to an extension of the account closure date and giving it enough time to find a new company willing to accept its business. This trend continued in the US, being first noticed by its banking regulators in 2005, with MSBs facing increasing difficulties to find a bank willing to conduct business with them, leading one regulator, in 2014, to issue a statement against this risk mitigation practice (Financial Crimes Enforcement Network 2014). Unable to retain a bank account and transfer money electronically, MSBs have turned to bulk cash couriers to move money across borders. The impact of derisking on MSBs in the US was raised by the US Comptroller of the Currency at a conference along with the worry that transactions "may be driven underground" as a result (Barry & Ensign 2016: n.p.).

At the national level, studies in the Caribbean found that in multiple territories MSBs had their bank accounts closed, blocking inbound remittances. A number of local banks also had their correspondent bank accounts closed, affecting the ability of their local customers to conduct international transactions (Wright 2016). A "stocktaking" exercise conducted by the Caribbean Financial Action Task Force in 2018–19 found that "low profit margins and the cost of compliance" was the main reason for terminating correspondent bank accounts (Pragg-Jaggernauth *et al.* 2019: 30). A related analysis was conducted by the Eastern and Southern Africa Anti-Money Laundering Group (ESAAMLG) in 2017, with a follow-up report in 2021. Their initial survey results found derisking in the form of terminated correspondent bank accounts and customer account closures throughout the region, with consequences for remittance flows and financial inclusion.[7] The extent of the impact of derisking across the region varied, but the reasons for terminating relationships were much the same as those found in the Caribbean, with the leading reason identified as a "Need to conform to regulatory enforcement obligations to avoid sanctions and reputational damage" (Working Group on Risk, Compliance and Financial Inclusion 2017: 48). The follow-up report found in the collected survey responses that the closure of correspondent banking and customer accounts continued for these same reasons.

The rational response in the banking industry (channelled through the FATF) that it is not reacting to the threat of sanctions for facilitating money laundering or terrorist financing but simply making a business decision is a bit disingenuous. What other factor, in addition to the AML/CFT compliance cost, has changed that makes a particular individual, business/charity, business sector or country too costly to service (and profit from)? These customer accounts were profitable before the risks and costs associated with them were increased by AML/CFT compliance. The fact that other financial firms have not replaced them demonstrates that the costs continue to exceed the potential profits, leading to the financial exclusion of individuals, businesses and effectively entire countries. The issue of derisking has come to be recognized as one element in the overall challenge of unintended consequences that arise from the actions of the FATF. In February 2021 the FATF began a project to explore the unintended consequences of "the incorrect implementation of the FATF Standards", including derisking, financial exclusion, and the impact on non-profit organizations and on human rights.[8] This study parallels work undertaken by the Royal United Services Institute (RUSI), funded by the Bill and Melinda Gates Foundation, investigating the impact of the AML/CFT regime on digital financial inclusion (Chase, van der Valk & Keatinge 2021). Aspects of these unintended consequences are discussed in the next two sections.

Charities and other non-profit organizations

Charities were immediately subjected to CFT measures (as explained in Chapter 3) because of al Qaida's use of charities to collect and transfer funds to the group. In turn, charities became one focus for FATF attention, specified in the initial CFT Special Recommendation 8, which was subsequently re-established as Recommendation 8 in the revised Forty Recommendations. In an analysis reflecting on the application of these CFT measures 15 years after they first came into force, Romaniuk and Keatinge pointed out that the first version of the Recommendation "contains an unsupported empirical claim – that NPOs are 'particularly vulnerable' – and asks states to ensure against their abuse on that basis. No evidence was offered at the time to justify this claim" (Romaniuk & Keatinge 2018: 268). The statement that some charities are vulnerable in terms of terrorist financing remains in the latest version of Recommendation 8. The guidance now encourages states to assess the measures applied to charities (non-profit organizations [NPOs] in FATF terminology) that may be misused for terrorist financing. Situating charities in the CFT regime in this fashion led to derisking in some states and oppressive regulation in other states, particularly where they were framed as the source of undesirable foreign influence in domestic society (Romaniuk & Keatinge 2018: 275; citing Hayes 2012: 10).

There are two issues present here: first, the problem that some domestic charities experienced with maintaining bank accounts; and second, the challenges confronting charities operating in or near conflict zones such as Syria with non-state actors named as terrorist groups. As discussed in the previous section, much of the attention given derisking involved MSBs and correspondent banking accounts. But charities also were subjected to derisking activity, and in the first years following publication of Special Recommendation 8 simply being an Islamic charity was sufficient reason for financial institutions to close their account. Because of the links made between charities and al Qaida, all domestic Islamic charities were suspect and treated as potentially financing terrorism, making them risky customers for a financial institution. Despite the implementation of CFT compliance measures by such charities, they continued to be affected by derisking actions, for example, the closure of Islamic Relief Worldwide's account by HSBC in 2015 (Keatinge & Keen 2017a: 12). As experienced by MSBs connected to *hawaladars*, the connection of a charity with an Islamic or Islamic-majority country was sufficient justification for closing its financial accounts to reduce the bank's risk of any future regulatory action against it.

In terms of the challenges faced by charities operating in or near conflict zones, in Somalia, for example, the impact of derisking is felt by local MSBs and charities. The few local banks are unable to arrange and maintain correspondent banking accounts, making it difficult for them to provide international transfers for MSBs and charities. This challenge is experienced by international aid agencies providing humanitarian aid as well, affecting money transfers to local projects and beneficiaries. Bankers in Somalia acknowledge the motivations behind derisking at international financial institutions, while some also view it as "an attack on Muslim nations" and "Islamophobic" because of the attention placed on Somalia (El Taraboulsi-McCarthy 2018: 7). A project at the Overseas Development Institute found that there was a negative impact from derisking across the Middle East region affecting humanitarian aid in several countries. In Yemen, the local conflict involves regional actors and some groups and individuals named as terrorists. To avoid the impact of derisking, Yemeni banks opened accounts with Chinese and European banks to avoid losing access to the international financial system in the event that US banks terminated all accounts linked to Yemen (El Taraboulsi-McCarthy & Cimatti 2018: 9). The conflict in Syria has received greater attention than Yemen, in part because of the emergence and spread of Islamic State in Iraq and the Levant (ISIL). Syria's banking system, however, was already subject to US sanctions before 2011, when the Syrian government's violent response to Arab Spring protests evolved into a civil war.[9] The subsequent spread of IS from Iraq into Syria brought international involvement, hampering the efforts of international humanitarian aid agencies. The experience of aid agencies and charities to provide their services without helping IS is explained further in Chapter 7.

In one study reflecting on 20 years of the AML/CFT regime and its evolution to incorporate informal economies the authors highlighted the "top-down"
structure of the FATF approach. Moreover, they observed that the focus on wire
transfers and charities reflected "the specifics of the terror finance threat landscape at the time" (2001) without appreciating the change that has also occurred
in the past 20 years (Keatinge & Keen 2020: vii). But the problem with establishing
an effective global AML/CFT regime is not limited to simply moving informal
transactions into the formal economy to track and trace them. Recognizing the
variability of risk factors present in any individual transaction or national political economy is only one aspect of the process. The RBA does not address some
of the other barriers that confront and prevent the introduction and implementation of AML/CFT legislation in some countries. A selection of these barriers
is presented in the next section, which reviews the actions taken by the FATF to
achieve establishment of a global AML/CFT regime.

FATF Recommendations: implementation and enforcement

The FATF established an approach for enforcing its AML Recommendations in
the 1990s, variously known as "naming and shaming" or "blacklisting" (Sharman
2009). The initial application of FATF enforcement measures, however, was
against states and non-independent territories that were not members of the
FATF. The FATF introduced its "non-cooperative countries and territories"
(NCCT) list to accompany a report published in 2000 highlighting the gaps in
its desired global regime to prevent and punish money laundering. The FATF
was assisted with enforcing the Recommendations by its associated regional
bodies and its guidance to treat any financial transaction with the listed territories as potentially criminal. This approach encouraged most of the named
territories to rapidly address the concerns raised by the FATF review of their
AML laws. Nonetheless, it was politically contentious for an international organization with limited membership to impose sanctions on non-member territories. The IMF and World Bank agreed to take on the evaluation of non-FATF
territories for compliance with the AML/CFT regime in 2004, with the explicit
understanding that they would not continue with blacklisting non-compliant
territories. The suspension of the FATF blacklist was temporary, and as already
discussed the FATF has resumed naming countries that are not compliant with
its Recommendations against money laundering and terrorist financing.

The experience of the Philippines with the NCCT blacklist is representative of the experience of other states evaluated by the FATF and assessed to
be insufficiently compliant with its Recommendations. The FATF found that
the Philippines did not have AML legislation in place in 2000, and it accused

the country of having "excessive secrecy provisions" covering financial records. Efforts to introduce AML legislation had been hampered by a domestic political economy that strongly desired bank secrecy to obfuscate the sources of election campaign funds and the profits of crony capitalism. When the country failed to immediately introduce AML legislation in 2001 the FATF threatened further countermeasures against financial transactions with the Philippines. Such measures would constrain the flow of migrant remittances, which contribute a significant amount to the national economy. Yet, it was the asset forfeiture provisions of the AML legislation that attracted the most resistance in the Philippine Congress, with politicians concerned that anyone convicted of a crime could have all their possessions seized. The FATF finally accepted the 2003 AML legislation implemented by the country at a meeting in 2005. The entire experience with the FATF over the NCCT list and its initial AML legislation would later influence regulations created for the mobile money industry and AML/CFT compliance in the Philippines. Mobile money emerged as a lower cost and quicker way to send remittances, and this new payment technology is discussed in more depth in Chapter 6.

The experience of states on the FATF blacklist at the beginning of the century served as an example to encourage other states to cooperate with an FATF assessment of their implementation of the AML/CFT regime. In 2010, for example, the mutual evaluation of Brazil's compliance with the Forty Recommendations was publicly released. In particular, the evaluation noted that terrorist financing had not been criminalized in Brazil, and its failure to correct this deficiency was raised at the FATF plenary meeting in February 2016. Further discussion occurred at the FATF meetings in June and October 2016, with the FATF acknowledging the progress made in Brazil to introduce and ratify legislation against terrorist financing. In October 2016 the decision at the FATF plenary meeting was to monitor the situation in Brazil for continued progress towards ratification and implementation of CFT legislation.[10] Brazil remained an agenda item at FATF meetings for the next three years. In part, the slow and deliberate action of the Brazilian government and legislature to introduce CFT legislation was due to the perception that terrorist financing is not a problem in Brazil, it is a problem in other countries. This perception is likely to be held by several countries without domestic terrorism and located at a distance from those countries experiencing transnational terrorism. Yet there was a further barrier to the introduction of CFT legislation that reflects Brazil's domestic political economy. While it had ratified the UN Convention for the Suppression of the Financing of Terrorism in 2005, the Brazilian experience shaped its approach to defining terrorism and preparing counterterrorism legislation. During the period from 2003 to 2016 senior members of the government, including the Brazilian president, belonged to the Workers' Party (Partido dos Trabalhadores).

The Workers Party and its members had been labelled as "terrorists" by the military dictatorship that ruled Brazil from 1964 to 1989, leaving them particularly sensitive over the application of the terrorist label to any individual or group (Lasmar 2019). Brazilian historical experience combined with a perception that it was not at risk from transnational terrorism and resulted in the slow progress towards implementing an FATF-compliant CFT regime.[11]

Beyond the view held in individual states regarding the presence or likelihood of terrorism (and thus terrorist financing activity), there is a broader, postcolonial, perspective that also influences states' definition of terrorism and terrorist financing.

> The African Union (AU), however, exempts decolonisation struggles for self-determination from its definition of terrorism. This highlights the fact that the definition of terrorism in Africa is contextualised within the political history of the continent. These differing perspectives indicate that although the definition of terror has been reconstructed by the AU, terror is not a novel phenomenon in Africa, neither is the financing of [the] same. (Azinge 2019: 246)

Transnational terrorist ideology, nonetheless, has influenced the conduct and practice of groups in Sub-Saharan Africa designated as terrorists by outside actors, such as Boko Haram in Nigeria. The Analytical Support and Sanctions Monitoring Team stated in its June 2021 Report that the "most striking development" of the first half of 2021 is that Africa was now the "region most affected by terrorism" (Analytical Support and Sanctions Monitoring Team 2021b: 5–6). In making that statement the report does not refer to Boko Haram, and instead refers to a number of groups linked to al Qaida and IS, reflecting its emphasis on transnational terrorism.[12] This disconnect between the emphasis of developed economies on transnational terrorism as compared to the informal economies that operate in much of the rest of the world in turn created the "regulatory misfit" that was identified in Nkechikwu Valerie Azinge's analysis of CFT in African states (Azinge 2019). It is similar to the regulatory misfit issue identified in relation to implementing money laundering legislation in Latin America with its range of informal economies (Thoumi & Anzola 2010).

The experience of the Philippines and Brazil demonstrates the argument of Fiona de Londras that the obligations of UN Security Council Resolutions serve to legislate changes to national CFT laws (de Londras 2019). The fact that these two states do so in direct response to FATF pressure situates the FATF as an agent of the UN Security Council. This relationship is entwined with the circular linkage between the original FATF Recommendation to ratify the UN Convention for the Suppression of the Financing of Terrorism and the Security Council Resolutions directing states to comply with the FATF Forty Recommendations. Another way to understand the experience of the Philippines and Brazil is offered by Shahar Hameiri and Lee Jones, who frame it as the introduction of global governance through the forced transformation of the state (Hameiri & Jones 2016). The Forty Recommendations provide guidance on the legal measures required for AML/CFT compliance that were crafted by the members of the FATF club for global implementation. To be assessed as compliant requires the enactment of domestic legislation that is then evaluated and determined consistent with FATF expectations. Yet another approach for understanding the creation of a global AML/CFT regime is an analysis that uses measurable values as representative indicators to produce an empirical analysis centred on "global performance indicators" (Morse 2019: 511). This analysis treats US power as flowing through foreign aid (a measurable variable) rather than through the imposition of substantial fines on foreign financial institutions and the application of sanctions intended to isolate the targeted state from the global financial system as the mechanisms for disciplining compliance.

These explanations for why states that were not members of the FATF subsequently joined a regional FATF-style organization and introduced AML/CFT legislation is immaterial to the conduct and operation of a global AML/CFT regime. The fact is that states have implemented some form of the FATF's regime and must now deal with the unintended consequences alongside its intended consequences. The disciplinary nature of the FATF's list of "High-risk and other monitored jurisdictions" is embodied in the actions taken by other states and international financial institutions to compel compliance with the FATF Forty Recommendations and so avoid becoming a monitored jurisdiction.

6

DEALING WITH NEW PAYMENT TECHNOLOGIES

"New payment technologies" was the term adopted by the FATF to identify emerging methods of payment in 1996. Today digital currencies and bitcoin immediately come to mind for the reader. Fifteen years ago, however, it was prepaid credit cards and e-gold that were of interest, with concerns surrounding their potential use in money laundering. The FATF study in 2006 was a follow up to the discussion of "Developments in New Technologies" included in the 1997 typologies report, reporting on presentations made to the group of experts by firms involved in electronic money (e-money) services.[1] The typologies meeting theme of e-money resulted from the 1996 revision to the Forty Recommendations, which introduced a new Recommendation 13 directing states to "pay special attention to money laundering threats in new and developing technologies that might favour anonymity". The latest version of the Forty Recommendations now addresses the topic in Recommendation 15, New Technologies, and broadens the scope of concern for AML/CFT to include new payment products, business practices and delivery systems.

In 1996, e-money was understood as either a stored value card, an internet-based system or a "hybrid system" combining features of these two technologies. The stored value or prepaid cards may carry the brand of a bank, Mastercard/Visa, a store or a money transfer firm. The customer places money on the card and then uses it just like they would a credit or debit card. As contactless technology has evolved, urban transportation systems have introduced the prepaid card in place of a ticket. In some cities the urban transportation system's card is also accepted for other payments, such as at a shop in the station. The early internet-based systems facilitated online payments and may have been linked to the customer's bank account. Although the passage of time means these early systems appear rudimentary today, in 1997 the FATF report described them as "sophisticated technologies", which is understandable when compared to the other payment methods available at the time. The discussion during the 1996 typologies meeting began with presentations from four industry organizations involved in providing these new financial technologies. The summary of the meeting included a request from these industry representatives for more information to understand the problem and to enable them to incorporate AML into their systems.

A decade later the FATF revisited the subject of new payment methods and noted the development of new technologies, along with an increase in the number of cross-border transactions supported by them. This report also noted the linkage that had been identified in the previous year's typologies report of the application of new payment methods to transfer migrant remittances. The 2006 typologies report investigates the evolution since the previous study of pre-paid cards and internet payment systems. It also looked at mobile payments and "digital precious metals" for compliance with the Forty Recommendations. The continued development and increased use of these payment systems brought further reports from the FATF, in 2008, 2010 and 2013, containing anonymized case studies to demonstrate the misuse of such systems for money laundering and terrorist financing. The latter report introduced an RBA methodology for these payment methods and identified the emergence of "decentralised digital currencies", with the possibility that anonymous access to them represented a money laundering/terrorist financing risk. The terminology for digital currencies was further specified by the FATF in 2014, supporting the application of AML/CFT to virtual currencies and demonstrated using case studies, including the takedown of the darknet website, Silk Road.

This chapter covers several of the new payment technologies and the measures implemented for applying the AML/CFT regime to them. Before covering specific payment technologies, the next section explains the underlaying structure that supports these and other payment systems. The second section explains the use of mobile phones and mobile money as payment systems, and the implementation of CDD in these technologies. The third section covers internet-based payment systems, including digital precious metals and the online payment system PayPal. Internet-based payment systems have evolved beyond supporting national currencies in the digital environment to supporting virtual assets, the term used by the FATF for digital currencies. These virtual assets are introduced in the fourth section. The final section of the chapter addresses the question of whether the future is cashless.

Payment system structures

Some concepts about money were introduced in Chapter 1: money as a medium of exchange, store of value and unit of account. In its cash form making a payment involves the physical exchange of the currency notes and coins for the desired good or service. Money has evolved from the physical currency notes issued by a ruler or government to physical abstractions such as cheques, money orders and credit/debit cards. More recently money has become the non-physical abstractions many of us use today, such as electronic bank transfers and transactions using our computers and mobile phones. This section provides an overview of payment systems as background for the new methods discussed in later sections. "A payment system is a set of instruments, procedures and rules for the transfer of funds among participants" (Bank for International Settlements 2020: 68). This background discussion on payment systems helps to identify where and when AML/CFT actions such as CDD occur when using a new method.

The payment system connecting an individual's credit or debit card to their account at a financial institution is a common one found across most economies. Your account details are read off the card by the merchant's point of sale (POS) device, either from a magnetic strip or a chip in the card. The POS device communicates with the merchant's payment processor, transmitting the transaction details with your account details to it. The payment processor contacts the financial institution requesting approval for paying the transaction, and when confirmed it will then provide approval back to the merchant's POS device. This final step will complete your transaction (Bank for International Settlements 2020: 70–75). Physical possession of the card, or for online transactions knowledge of the card verification value (CVV) printed on the card, demonstrates you are either the owner of the account or that you are an authorized user of the account. The financial institution that maintains the account and issued the card is responsible for completing CDD as part of its AML/CFT compliance. Every merchant accepting the card for payment is relying on the financial firm to complete the CDD process correctly so that they are not accused of facilitating money laundering or terrorist financing. Consequently, everyone goes through a customer identity verification process when opening a financial account, and in some countries they may have to go through a periodic re-verification process. Any company providing a financial account without conducting the CDD step will be violating local AML/CFT regulations.

There are a number of other payment systems that overlay the system used by credit/debit cards. They do so by linking their process to the individual's credit/debit card, or in some cases directly to the individual's bank account. This method of linking to your credit/debit card, for example, is used by Apple Pay and Google Pay.[2] In both systems they know your credit/debit card details, but when you use your phone to make a payment they provide a separate, unique identifier for you to the merchant's POS device. The transaction information is collected by the mobile phone app, which then communicates with your financial institution for approval and transmits confirmation of the approval back to the merchant's device. As pointed out by both Apple and Google, their method keeps the individual's specific card details private from the merchant. Neither Apple nor Google, however, are performing CDD; instead they are relying on the issuer of the card to have completed it.

Possession of a credit/debit card had been predicated on possessing a financial institution account before the introduction of the prepaid credit/debit card. While the stored value card is available in several forms, prepaid credit/debit cards are popular for their almost universal acceptance when carrying the brand of a major credit/debit card service provider (e.g. Mastercard or Visa). A payment processor or financial firm holds the monetary value placed on the card and services the transactions applied to it, with the account itself generally being tracked against the card details. Information about the card holder is not collected until the card is registered, meaning that it is possible to possess and use a prepaid card anonymously. As an example, a prepaid card available at a large American retail store allowed the customer to initially load up to $500 on a card without providing identification. To add more than $500 to the card at the time of purchase, or to add more value (reload) the card at a later date, required that it be registered and identification details collected, completing a CDD process. The maximum amount that could be held on the card was $3,000, helping to reduce the risk of misuse of the card for money laundering. At the same time, an individual could visit multiple stores and place the maximum $500 in cash on a prepaid card without providing ID.[3] In this way the individual could transform a large quantity of cash into a stack of prepaid debit cards, but it is not a convenient method to use for large-scale and recurring money laundering activity. Some prepaid cards have been marketed at migrant workers to support sending home remittances. These cards have a "partner" card that is sent to the intended recipient of the remittances to enable them to withdraw funds using the card at their location after money has been loaded to it by the migrant worker. This method for sending migrant remittances, however, has largely been replaced by mobile money, discussed in the next section. Prepaid cards were found in the possession of the terrorist attackers in Paris in 2015, leading the French government to propose increased regulation of them (Stothard 2015).

Some electronic and online transactions involve the credit/debit card transaction payment structure, either by directly using the card or by overlaying the structure (see more on Paypal later). Other online transactions may involve the bank-to-bank system, such as moving money from an account you have at one financial institution to an account at a second financial institution (e.g. to pay rent or for child care). Bank-to-bank systems may cover financial institutions within a single country (e.g. Automated Clearing House (ACH) in the US), a currency area (e.g. Single Euro Payments Area (SEPA) in the eurozone) or cross-border transfers via SWIFT, a leading international financial messaging system.[4]

Some online transactions may operate through a hybrid structure involving aspects of both the credit/debit card payment process and the bank-to-bank payment process. An online foreign currency transfer service, for example, may withdraw money from your bank account as a debit card transaction and then make the transfer to deposit the foreign currency amount in the receiving bank account via the bank-to-bank payment system. In this example, the foreign currency transfer service may perform its own "know your customer" process in addition to the CDD process that it knows the bank conducted when you opened your account.

A further feature enabled by the use of new payment methods was noted in the 2010 FATF study: the fact that use of an electronic payment system leads to the production of an "electronic trace" of the transaction. Even where the transaction may be effectively anonymous because CDD was not performed, such as with the purchase of a prepaid debit card with no more than $500 in cash, using that card produced an electronic record of the transaction. In turn, that electronic trace would be available for law enforcement if needed to support an investigation. Anonymity, however, is desired by more than simply those engaged in illicit activity trying to conceal their illicit conduct. It is also desired by those avoiding state surveillance for other, legitimate, reasons. The asylum seeker, for example, that desires to send money back to friends and family without revealing themselves to the government of where they now live and have gained sanctuary. In this situation they want the transaction to be anonymous to protect themselves and their friends and family from government reprisals.

Mobile phones and mobile money

It is important to understand that mobile money is distinct and different from mobile banking and mobile phone payment methods such as Apple Pay and Google Pay. As explained in the previous section, the latter two mobile phone payment methods overlay an existing financial account linked to a credit/debit card. Similarly, mobile banking is the use of a mobile phone app to access and use a retail financial account. Mobile money, on the other hand, operates through the mobile phone network and is independent of a traditional retail financial account. For precision, the Groupe Spéciale Mobile Association (GSMA) details the following regarding what mobile money is:

• it is a service that transfers money, makes payments and receives payments with a mobile phone;
• it is a service that is available to everyone, including people without a retail bank account;

- it is a service that is widely accessible through a network of agents; and
- it is *not* a service that provides access to a retail bank account, credit card or mobile payment service connected to a retail bank account or credit card (for example, Apple Pay and Google Wallet).

(Naghavi 2020: 65)

The GSMA was established in 1982 and grew to be the international organization that represents companies involved in the mobile phone technology industry.[5] While this definition excludes access to retail bank accounts, the companies that provide mobile money services are increasingly integrating access to bank accounts to extend their customer base (Naghavi 2020: 24–6).

One genealogy for the development of mobile money traces it to the early twenty-first century practice of migrants purchasing mobile phone top-up credit for the mobile phone network used by family and friends in their country of origin. They would then either send the physical top-up card or just the codes from the top-up card to the intended recipient. The top-up value could then either be applied to a mobile phone account or resold for local currency, with the money then used for other purposes. This practice represented yet another form of informal value transfer supporting migrant remittances, a practice that emerged alongside the global spread of mobile phone technology. This method for sending money home would be formalized by mobile phone companies themselves with the creation of the mobile money service, which is generally attributed to the introduction of M-Pesa in 2007 by Safaricom in Kenya and by Vodacom in Tanzania (Maurer 2012: 595).

These early mobile money systems operated through the mobile phone company using text messages. Transactions involved moving credit from one customer account with the mobile money operator (MMO) to the customer account of the recipient. Initially both accounts had to be with the same MMO, and for the company it was a bookkeeping exercise rather than a financial or banking transaction. This structure led to a perception that the MMO was not required to perform CDD on its customers; a perception that led one commentator in the US to postulate a scenario in which mobile money was used for terrorist financing. The scenario involved the use of an anonymous stored value card, a disposable mobile phone and a generic email account to register the phone number with the MMO. The money on the stored value card would be uploaded to the mobile money account associated with the phone number and then transferred to the intended recipient. Naturally the recipient would have established their account with a disposable mobile phone registered with a generic email address. Even at the time, however, it was a potential misuse of mobile money that was not possible with the MMOs in operation because they were all performing CDD on their customers. Anonymous registration of a mobile money account was not possible because the process involved presenting ID to an agent of the MMO to open an account. In addition, to reduce the risk of money laundering with mobile money, MMOs had limits on the size of an individual transaction, on the total amount that could be transferred in a day and month, and on the total amount permitted in an account.

The mobile money industry has evolved alongside mobile phone technology. From MMS text messages on the feature phones widely in use in 2010, MMOs also now work with an app for smart phones, providing enhanced security features and additional capabilities. From its origins as a method for simply transferring money between two customers, mobile money is now used to pay bills and taxes, receive wages and government benefits, and to access other financial services including savings accounts, loans and insurance (Naghavi 2020: 32–7). Interoperability extends beyond retail bank accounts to include other MMOs, expanding the customer base and range of agencies and businesses utilizing mobile money services. Consequently, mobile money has come to be identified as a tool for achieving greater financial inclusion. The inclusion of AML/CFT in the mobile money industry is recognized as necessary, in particular the requirement for a CDD process. But the CDD process also represents a barrier to entry for accessing financial services, as discussed in Chapter 5. This situation produces a dilemma for those specialists approaching mobile money as a route to increased financial inclusion when some of the same barriers continue to be present, for example, the need for a government-approved identity document and a fixed, physical address. A GSMA study in 2019 explored these challenges and offered several proposals for resolving them (Kipkemboi, Woodsome & Pisa 2019). As with several other areas affected by the Covid-19 pandemic, the CDD process for mobile money was simplified to incorporate physical distancing while account limits were raised to handle an increased demand for mobile money services (Bazarbash *et al.* 2020).

The simplified CDD measures introduced in response to the pandemic in 2020 built on existing experience with introducing an RBA to mobile money as one way to increase financial inclusion. In addition to India's Aadhaar ID system (discussed in Chapter 5), Colombia and Pakistan have implemented a national biometric identification system. These systems can then be used to support the CDD process in the opening of a mobile money account and in mobile phone SIM registration processes.[6] Simplifying the CDD process for mobile money does not appear to have increased the use of mobile money for money laundering or terrorist financing. None of the cases described by the FATF in its December 2020 update on money laundering and terrorist financing (made to reflect changes introduced to CDD process as a result of the pandemic) involved mobile money. Perhaps more importantly, none of the cases identified in the report concerned terrorist financing, only money laundering. The situation in 2020 remained similar to the experience of a decade earlier, when the case studies involving new payment methods were not related to terrorist financing but only money laundering. Nevertheless, performance of CDD data collection by the MMO does not assure that names are verified against UN sanctions lists, nor that they are checked against a national list of suspected terrorist actors. There is also no assurance that local, small-scale terrorist financing cannot occur, as small-scale local acts of terrorism often do not require a lot of money.

Internet-based payment systems

Digital precious metals are one of the earliest forms of digital financial asset and internet-based payment systems, starting with the establishment of the e-gold, Ltd Company in 1996 (Mullan 2014: 21). In 2006 the FATF described internet payment systems as those which use the internet to transfer payment between banks accounts, or those non-bank companies that do not require a bank account that provide payment services. The former internet payment system is better understood as internet or mobile banking, as mentioned in the previous section. The latter non-bank service "may not be subject to the same AML/CFT measures that apply to banks", which concerned the FATF. The report continued by identifying PayPal as the most widely used non-bank internet payment system. Digital precious metals were treated as a separate payment method in this report, which named e-gold as the "oldest and best known" example of it. When the FATF revisited this topic in 2010 the category of internet payment system was updated to include online banking, "prepaid internet payment products" and digital currencies. Online banking was considered beyond the scope of the analysis and not mentioned in the remainder of the FATF document. Digital currencies included both currencies and precious metals, whereas prepaid products were identified as methods used by companies that transferred funds for customers using an internet-accessible prepaid account.

The story of e-gold is instructive for the operation of internet payment systems because it continues to be referenced in discussions of virtual currencies. Indicted for money laundering in 2007, the founder pled guilty in 2008 in a plea deal.[7] Like the originator of the concept behind bitcoin, the founder of e-gold, Ltd, has a political-economic mission. In essence, the objective was to establish a gold-based money that operated independently of governments yet would be available to everyone via the internet (Mullan 2014: 26). At the turn of the century, the regulation of internet-based financial services was limited or non-existent. P. Carl Mullan writes that the e-gold website was populated with disclaimers stating that e-gold was not a bank (2014: 27). Additionally, because it was explicitly a payment system and not a money transmitting service, the company believed that regulations on money transmitters (MSBs) did not apply to e-gold (Zetter 2009). The US government disagreed with the company's analysis of the law and, in addition to the money laundering charge, the indictment included charges of operating an unlicensed money transmitting business and transmitting money without a license (Doherty 2021: 23).

As with traditional gold standard currencies, the owner of an e-gold account possessed an electronic claim on that quantity of gold. The currency in which the account was denominated was independent of the specific quantity of digital gold credited to the account. The quantity of "digital gold" existed in "physical gold" held in a gold repository for the company (Mullan 2014: 22–3). As the company grew it became necessary to shift from gold coins and ingots secured in the company's Florida office to gold bars stored in gold repositories in London and Dubai (Zetter 2009). The e-gold customer could acquire and spend fractional quantities of a gold ingot. This approach made the payment services accessible to anyone because they were not limited to acquiring entire gold coins or ingots. And this structure made spending the digital currency equally accessible, achieved by spending a relatively small amount of currency backed by a fraction of a gold ingot. The feature that made e-gold popular with retailers is that all payments were instantaneous and final, no amount of buyer remorse could enable a customer to ask for their money back (Mullan 2014: 22–3). The feature that made e-gold popular for illicit payments was the fact that limited CDD was initially conducted. The company believed that AML/CFT requirements did not apply to their business.[8] Subsequent efforts to improve the company's CDD procedures following news media reports on e-gold's popularity with criminals were not enough to avoid the indictment and conviction of the company's owners (Zetter 2009). Although other digital assets have gained more public attention than gold and other precious metals, the use of gold as a store of value and unit of exchange for illegal purposes remains an area of interest for the FATF.

PayPal was created as an internet payment system that processed transactions for users of the eBay online auction website. It was bought by eBay in 2002 and remained part of the corporation until 2015, when PayPal was spun off as a separate, independent payment processing company once again (Jackson 2004).[9] Originally PayPal accounts were only connected to an individual's credit card or bank account. As a result, the company was relying on the bank or credit card issuer to perform CDD for compliance requirements. This approach is consistent with the survey results reported by the FATF in 2010: not all jurisdictions stating that they hosted an internet payment service company required them to be licensed or registered. PayPal would introduce its own CDD process following allegations in the US of money laundering and facilitating fraud, along with processing payments for online gambling in 2002 when online gambling was still illegal throughout the US. Support for the online gambling industry, however, was terminated in 2002 by eBay at the time it acquired PayPal (Jackson 2004).

Today a PayPal account may be opened using an email address without linking the account to a credit/debit card or bank account at first. This process opens an "unverified" account, which comes with limits on the amount of money that it can send, receive and withdraw.[10] To work with more money in the account it must be verified by PayPal, which requires the account owner to provide details on a credit/debit card or bank account. This information is used by PayPal to confirm the identity of the account owner and comply with CDD requirements. In some cases further identification documents may be necessary to comply with local regulations.[11]

In 2004 PayPal reached a settlement agreement with the Department of Justice over the allegations made that it had supported online gambling (McCullagh 2004). Much like several international financial service firms over the past decade, PayPal has been charged with weak AML/CFT compliance and violating US sanctions. For example, in 2015 PayPal agreed to a settlement over accusations of violating US sanctions against Cuba, Iran and Sudan. The US Treasury Department had identified "nearly 500 PayPal transactions, worth almost $44,000, [that] potentially violated U.S. sanctions" over a period of several years (Ensign 2015: n.p.). As is common in such cases, PayPal neither admitted nor denied the allegations when making this settlement agreement with the government (Ensign 2015). The company was accused of terrorist financing alongside bitcoin in a 2017 newspaper article reporting on information released by the Indonesian Financial Transaction Reports and Analysis Center. The transactions allegedly "supported terror cells across Indonesia, largely in Java", though because of limited internet access outside of urban areas, the funds were cashed out once accessed by the PayPal user in Indonesia (Yuniar 2017: n.p.). With few details provided in the newspaper article, a more complete picture emerges in a conference paper drawing on confidential interviews. An individual in Syria used PayPal to transfer funds to an individual in Indonesia, who then transferred it to the local bank account of an IS sympathizer. The money was then provided to a bomb maker and suicide bomber to cover expenses and compensation for the bomber's widow (Jusi, Satrya & Wardoyo 2019: 305–6). As an example of terrorist finance using an internet-based payment system, this case from Indonesia demonstrates once again the challenges in effective AML/CFT enforcement. The small quantities of money involved are concealed among the large number of legitimate small transactions taking place every day.

Virtual assets

The desire for anonymity is a leading motivation for the development and use of bitcoin and other digital assets. The development of digital assets, denominated in a fiat currency but not in the physical possession of the owner/investor, predates the release of the bitcoin concept paper in 2008.[12] As discussed in the previous section, digital precious metals may be the earliest form of a virtual financial asset, as seen with the establishment of e-gold, Ltd in 1996. The more well-known digital currencies, such as bitcoin, represent what the FATF has defined as "virtual assets", that is, the "digital representation of value" that may be sold, traded or transferred as a form of payment or investment. Virtual assets are included in the Forty Recommendations as part of Recommendation 15 on new payment technologies. The FATF definition is intentionally broad in scope to cover all existing as well as future digital financial instruments that could be misused for money laundering and terrorist financing. The cross-border potential of virtual assets (as with all internet-based payment methods) means that individuals may have access to them even when the local government has expressly banned them (e.g. as in China in 2021). The challenge when banning virtual assets is the same as that faced when making any activity illegal: if demand for it continues to exist the activity moves to the underground economy and beyond the view of AML/CFT surveillance methods. Consequently, the RBA guidance document for virtual assets encourages countries that prohibit virtual assets and virtual asset service providers to continue to include them in their risk assessment for AML/CFT compliance because residents may still access and use foreign service providers for illicit purposes.

Rather than provide a comprehensive description of virtual assets in all their variety, an explanation of a singular cryptocurrency should be sufficient. The cryptocurrency exists as a digital record representing a quantity of that cryptocurrency, whether it is bitcoin, dogecoin, ethereum, tether, etc. The value of an individual unit of the cryptocurrency in fiat currency (e.g. US dollars) may vary based on the demand, as with bitcoin, or it may be fixed to the value of another asset, as in the case of tether, which is fixed to the US dollar.[13] The latter structure for valuing a cryptocurrency is also known as being a stablecoin, because it is fixed, and it is intended to facilitate the cryptocurrency to operate as a reliable medium of exchange (Houben & Snyers 2020: 20). The owner of a cryptocurrency possesses their units of cryptocurrency in a digital wallet that is protected for the owner through encryption and the use of passwords. The digital wallet could be stored on a portable USB device separate from any specific computer. Thus, possession of the wallet and relevant passwords gives one possession of the cryptocurrency stored in that wallet. Transactions involving the cryptocurrency are recorded and the record maintained publicly to ensure that any unit of cryptocurrency is possessed by a single user and cannot be used in more than one transaction (which transfers "ownership" of that unit).

The ownership and use of a cryptocurrency can be somewhat anonymous when there is no identifiable information about the owner of the wallet associated with it. It also requires the user to take measures to disguise the IP address associated with the device holding the wallet from which the transaction originates and is completed if they wish to remain anonymous (Mullan 2014: 89–92). Such anonymity is a problem for AML/CFT, leading to FATF guidance on registration, licensing and user CDD, along with work carried out by individual governments to track the units of cryptocurrency connected to or involved with criminal activity. The FATF provides one example of the involvement of cryptocurrency in criminal activity on their website, which involves the virtual assets used in the 2017 "Wannacry" ransomware attack. In this instance the hackers were unable to complete the process to convert the bitcoins collected from the ransom into a fiat currency.[14] The FATF graphic present on its website (see note 14) includes the layering stage pursued to transform the cryptocurrency identification data of the ransom bitcoins into cryptocurrency bitcoins from other sources, a process known as mixing or tumbling (Campbell-Verduyn 2018: 298).[15] Making the transaction record longer and more complex as a layering methodology to obfuscate the illegal origin of a quantity of cryptocurrency may not succeed, as seen in the FATF's example. In addition to this example, the techniques used by law enforcement to trace and seize the virtual assets associated with criminal activities, such as the Silk Road online marketplace case and with other ransomware attacks are widely described in news reports.

Publicly available information on the actual use of virtual assets for terrorist financing, on the other hand, is limited. One example was the reference to bitcoin and "virtual money" made by the chairman of the Indonesian Financial Transaction Reports and Analysis Center in 2017 (Yuniar 2017: n.p.). Another example is the 2020 US Department of Justice announcement about its seizure of cryptocurrency from wallets connected to three terrorist organizations. The "three terror finance cyber-enabled campaigns" named in the press release had intended to raise funds for the military wing of Hamas (al-Qassam Brigades), and for al Qaida and IS (Office of Public Affairs 2020). Details of the fundraising activity and cryptocurrency donations for the first two groups were publicized in a series of blog articles in 2019 by Elliptic, a company providing compliance services to the virtual assets industry.[16] In addition to information on the al-Qassam Brigades fundraising campaign, the first Elliptic blog article related another group's fundraising efforts that netted $1,037 in bitcoin over eighteen months (Carlisle 2019). The company then provided more information in a later blog article, stating that the al-Qassam Brigades had collected thousands of dollars in bitcoin donations. But Elliptic also observed that this same bitcoin account had "received over $100,000 in cryptocurrency from other sources" (Wilder 2019: n.p.). At the time that the Department of Justice closed down these fundraising activities it had "seized millions of dollars, over 300 cryptocurrency accounts, four websites and four Facebook pages" (Office of Public Affairs 2020: n.p.). Hamas and the al-Qassam Brigades continue to solicit cryptocurrency donations, with an increase of donations reported following the May 2021 conflict in Gaza (Coles & Faucon 2021).

The current regulatory environment is far different from the situation when e-gold was founded and internet payment systems were novel. The obligation for AML/CFT compliance has been clear for more than a decade and virtual assets have been explicitly included in the scope of AML/CFT by the FATF. Yet in 2019 Facebook announced a new digital payment method, releasing a white paper describing this new virtual asset environment but failing to include AML/CFT compliance (Libra Association 2019). In much the same way that the founder of e-gold felt AML/CFT regulations would not apply because it was not an MSB, the Facebook vice-president responsible for Libra asserted that banking regulations would not apply because "we're not a bank" (Waters & Murphy 2019: n.p.). Originally named Libra, the new cryptocurrency would be a stablecoin, backed by hard assets with a constant value. A subsidiary separate from Facebook would be established with several partners to oversee this new virtual asset and its supporting wallet. And one of the goals for this new cryptocurrency was to provide financial services to the unbanked, helping them "to save some of the $25 billion 'lost by migrants every year through remittance fees'" (Horwitz & Olson 2019: n.p.). From a financial inclusion perspective it is a worthy goal and welcome. But as is clear from earlier discussions of financial inclusion and migrant remittances, the AML/CFT obligation for CDD procedures remain part of the environment.

Regulators and other government officials did not agree with the expectations of Facebook and the Libra project team. In addition to their concern that Libra represented a risk for money laundering and terrorist financing, they also raised a concern that it and other cryptocurrencies could be a threat to financial stability and government monetary policy. In response to the scrutiny, Facebook reassessed the Libra project, with their first step being to establish a clear separation between the social media company and the association governing it. The cryptocurrency was renamed Diem, the oversight association was reorganized and renamed the Diem Association (its membership also shrank to 27 participants, down from the initial goal of 100 members of the association), and Diem would now be a stablecoin linked to the US dollar (Kharif 2020).[17] The new approach is outlined in a revised white paper, which now contains a clear explanation for the inclusion of AML/CFT procedures in the design and operation of Diem as a payment system (Libra Association 2020). At the time of writing, the Diem stablecoin is not yet in operation.

Is the future cashless?

The global pandemic that began in 2020 encouraged a shift away from cash in many places, in part due to a fear that the virus could be transmitted through contact with currency. The pandemic accelerated a trend in some economies, while in others, where the use of cash had retained dominance, the switch to using a card was strongly encouraged because of the pandemic (Arnold 2020). This pandemic-induced shift in consumer habits serves to support the argument for a cashless society. For more than two decades some have argued that cash, particularly the high denomination notes, should be eliminated because it is central to the illegal economy. The economist Kenneth Rogoff, for example, argues that removing these notes from circulation will help to combat corruption, drug trafficking, human trafficking, tax evasion and terrorism (Rogoff 2016). A similar argument is made by Peter Sands. His analysis emphasized the use of high denomination notes from major international currencies (euro, Swiss franc, Japanese yen, British pound, Canadian dollar and US dollar) in other countries' illegal economies (Sands 2016). The increased use of the $100 note outside of the US was commented on by the IMF in 2019, who noted that 80 per cent of these notes were circulating in foreign countries (International Monetary Fund 2019). The latter situation is quite understandable in places where there is little trust in the local currency.

For the foreseeable future, however, this trend towards a cashless society will be predominantly a developed economy phenomenon. Yet even in these countries there remains a segment of the population that relies on cash. Elsewhere, in cash-based economies, and especially those with large informal economic sectors, this trend will be constrained by local economic circumstances. Although alternatives to cash, such as mobile money and internet payment systems, will grow in usage, these alternatives require a supporting infrastructure of electricity and internet access to operate efficiently. As already mentioned, the FATF supports and encourages financial inclusion because it moves people from a cash-only economy to one involving payment methods subjected to AML/CFT surveillance. Although it may enhance financial surveillance against terrorist financing, the shift away from the anonymity of cash also reinforces existing concerns about personal privacy and the use of this surveillance data for other purposes by governments. And without legislation to remove the possibility for anonymity that remains with some non-cash payment methods, it may not effectively limit all terrorist financing. As mentioned earlier the terrorists behind the Paris attacks in November 2015 used prepaid cards acquired anonymously. Subsequently the French government called for tighter regulations on prepaid cards to prevent their anonymous purchase and use (Stothard 2015).

The desire for anonymity is not limited to promoters of bitcoin, criminals and terrorists. Ordinary citizens also have any number of reasons to keep an individual transaction private, for example, to keep the purchase of a gift from appearing in the online transaction list for a joint credit/debit card. Moreover, cash does not rely on an underlying infrastructure to be used in a transaction. If the card network or electricity grid is down, cards and mobile phone payment apps fail while cash may still be accepted by a merchant. An experience with these problems provides one reason for an increase in cash hoarding, such as was seen during the pandemic. Consequently, the desire of the FATF and its member countries to make all economic transactions visible and traceable conflicts with individual desires, both licit and illicit, for privacy and anonymous economic relations. Police reports on the use of bitcoin for money laundering provide one reflection of these desires: "'While cash still remains king in the criminal word [sic], as digital platforms develop we're increasingly seeing organised criminals using cryptocurrency to launder their dirty money,' said the Metropolitan police's deputy assistant commissioner, Graham McNulty" (*The Guardian* 2021: n.p.). As directed in Recommendation 15, new payment technologies must be assessed for the risk that they may be misused for money laundering and terrorist financing. And the necessary measures to implement and comply with AML/CFT obligations need to be part of their design and operation. Cash, however, will remain a challenge for AML/CFT efforts.

7

THE FINANCING OF ISLAMIC STATE

Among the enduring images of Islamic State's time controlling territory in Iraq and Syria are photographs and videos of the wanton destruction of the ancient ruins of Palmyra. From the perspective of its strict adherence to a Salafi-jihadist branch of Islam, these historic sites were idolatrous, justifying this massive act of iconoclasm. Other examples that were recorded and shared by the group included the destruction of items at the Mosul Cultural Museum, the Nineveh archaeological site and the Nimrud archaeological site (González Zarandona, Albarrán-Torres & Isakhan 2018). At the same time, this iconoclasm concealed a conscious material motivation to acquire portable relics and antiquities for sale on the black market, which provided a further source of income. The multitude of income sources utilized by IS attracted the attention of the governments working to counter this new transnational terrorist threat. The UN Security Council directed the production of a report by the Analytical Support and Sanctions Monitoring Team specifically on IS in 2014. Subsequently, the FATF and a number of other organizations produced additional studies analysing IS finances and suggesting methods to prevent its fundraising as a way of defeating the group.

IS, also known as Islamic State of Iraq and Syria (ISIS) and Islamic State of Iraq and the Levant (ISIL), as well as by the Arabic acronym, Daesh, succeeded in controlling territory across Iraq and Syria for a period from 2014 to 2019 (Talley & Faucon 2020). As such, it offers a case study that is different from other twenty-first-century terrorist groups, with its capacity to exploit different sources of funding, including oil and taxation. Simultaneously, it provides a case study for assessing the effectiveness of the tools used to combat the financing of terrorism. The next section introduces IS, explaining its evolution out of a series of earlier jihadist groups in the region and the ways that it collected revenue before 2014. The second section explores the funding methods that controlling territory allowed IS, meaning they were able to gather revenue "like a state". This is followed by a companion section covering the other methods used by an insurgent/terrorist group that also continued to be used by IS. The final section looks at the threat posed by IS following 2019 and its continued capacity for violence, supported by the assets it was able to gather while controlling territory in Iraq and Syria.

The origins and starting capital of Islamic State

Analysing IS as an ideology, Fawaz A. Gerges situated the group within a genealogy of Salafi-jihadist tradition that is older than its predecessor, al Qaida. IS harkens back to "a narrow, strict, and obsolete textualist reading of Islamic doctrine" to shape a religious community for a new caliphate (Gerges 2016: 26–7). This reading of Islamic doctrine serves the group as justification to "purify" its territory of those that do not practice its form of Islam and the objects (antiquities and historic sites) that represent forms of idolatry (Gerges 2016: 30). While these actions may be disturbing in the eyes of many people, the ideological message promulgated by IS was appealing to some viewers. To an extent not seen since the 1980s and resistance to the Soviet occupation of Afghanistan had a group attracted so many foreign recruits. IS's claim to represent the most correct form of Islam and to provide a secure place in which to practice it attracted so many foreign fighters that it raised concerns among government officials and the UN Security Council (Gerges 2016: 43–7). It is important to recognize that IS's pursuit of territorial control was, however, a different trajectory from al Qaida and its other affiliated groups, as well as other groups pursuing the Salafi-jihadist view of politics.

Organizationally, IS was previously Islamic State in Iraq, which the group declared itself to be in 2006 as one among several militias and insurgent groups operating in Iraq at the time. This group had earlier identified itself as al Qaida in Iraq, following its rebranding in 2004 of the group Jama'at al-Tawhid wal-Jihad (founded in 1999) as the local al Qaida franchise (Mohamedou 2018: 88–100).[1] It is important to recognize the landscape in which this evolution took place, which led IS to adopt a strategy of seizing territory across Iraq and Syria and exercising governance over it: in May 2011 Osama bin Laden was killed by US special forces in Pakistan; the US military completed the withdrawal of its forces from Iraq in December 2011; and governments across the Middle East were unsettled by the protests that erupted in 2011, known as the Arab Spring. In Iraq, the Shia-led central government engaged in sectarian violence that encouraged the growth of Sunni militias, including Islamic State in Iraq. One outcome of this violence was that it left the group with "only the most battle-hardened elements of AQI and ISI standing" (Mohamedou 2018: 94). In Syria the Arab Spring protests germinated into a civil uprising that became a civil war involving multiple groups against the central government. It is in the midst of these events that IS shifted from al Qaida's transnational model of franchises to a new transnational model of regions, creating "an organic rather than a decentralised entity" (Mohamedou 2018: 89). Combining this model with territorial control of a region allowed IS to move away from al Qaida's original model of financing through donations and to become self-sufficient by either taxing or confiscating the resources of the region (Mohamedou 2018: 109–10).

The control of territory for IS began with the group establishing itself as the dominant insurgent group in northeast Syria, near the border with Iraq, in early 2014. From this base it moved to take control of adjacent territory in Iraq, prominently seizing Iraq's second largest city, Mosul, with little resistance in June 2014 (Mohamedou 2018: 98–9). The "shock and awe" experienced in Western capitals following this event comes from the fact that in just four days some 1,500 IS fighters had swept away the 32,000 members of Iraqi military and police forces responsible for defending the city (Mohamedou 2018: 120; Al-Salhy & Arango 2014). A RAND report collected together information on IS in the public domain prior to 2012. In part this report sought to dispel the notion that the "reemergence" of IS in 2014 should have been unexpected. Rather, the group, "its methods and goals, should not come as a surprise" because it reflected the evolution of IS over the preceding two decades (Shatz & Johnson 2015: 1). The rapidity with which it gained control of several major cities and their surrounding areas in 2014 was also due to circumstances: IS accomplished this feat because the governments of Iraq and Syria were struggling with civil uprisings and civil war, in part influenced by external actors. Suppressing IS and evicting it from territorial control would require the further intervention of other foreign actors who had deployed their military to support Iraqi and Syrian government forces, while also supporting several local ethnic-based militia groups (Mohamedou 2018: 120).

The RAND report further explained how, pre-2014, IS and its precursor groups were different from al Qaida because of their source of funding. The point of difference highlighted by Shatz and Johnson was that IS's funding was local rather than foreign, a conclusion that "contradicts the persistent misperception that wealthy Persian Gulf donors were important funders of the group" (Shatz & Johnson 2015: 8). Locally sourced income came from oil smuggling, selling stolen merchandise and extortion. Essentially the group was operating like an organized criminal gang to finance its insurgent agenda (Shatz & Johnson 2015: 8–9). The figure widely reported about IS's financial position before taking control of Mosul was that it possessed "total cash and assets" worth $875 million (Chulov 2014: n.p.). Naturally, its ability to engage in criminal conduct at this scale expanded further once it had gained control of the territory. For example, it was reported that IS seized the contents of bank vaults throughout Mosul, including some $425 million from the Mosul branch of the Iraq Central Bank (McCoy 2014). This report was contradicted by an article in the *Financial Times* a month later that cited bank executives in Iraq declaring that no banks were robbed in Mosul and that the banks continued to operate as normal (Daragahi 2014).[2]

The perception that IS emerged unexpectedly in 2014 to become the major international concern over stability in the Middle East was widespread. The first of many UN Security Council Resolutions involving IS was released on 15 August 2014. Resolution 2170 (2014) condemned the group's actions in Iraq and Syria and directed the Monitoring Team to provide a report addressing the threat posed by IS for the region. In response to IS's "rapid development", the FATF produced a new study of terrorist finance specifically focused on the group. Building on the FATF's previous analysis of terrorist financing, the starting premise for the study was that IS "represents a new form of terrorist organisation where funding is central and critical to its activities".[3] This premise exposes a fundamental conceit for discussions of the funding behind IS during the years that it controlled territory. It is a claim that IS represented a new and different set of circumstances for the international regime against terrorist financing. The additional sources of funding listed by the FATF, such as extorting fees on goods in transit, are because of the fact that IS controlled territory. The situation was like that of other insurgent groups who controlled territory, including FARC and LTTE as discussed in Chapter 2. Stepping back from simply understanding this activity through the framework of IS as a terrorist organization, the activity named in the study as extortion is called taxation and the collection of tariffs when it is performed by a government. This fact is recognized later in the FATF study when it lists "illicit taxation of goods and cash" as one of the sources of funding for IS.

Furthermore, the FATF study's reference to IS operating similar to an organized crime group echoes the argument of Charles Tilly: that state making represents the highest form of organized crime (Tilly 1985). Yet with control of territory comes the responsibility to govern those inhabiting that territory, whether it is by an elected government or by an insurgent group. One contemporary news report pointed out that US government officials should have understood the different financing capabilities available to IS from its control of territory. Over the preceding decade these officials should have gained experience from dealing with "other extremist groups that had gained control of territory", including the al Qaida franchise in Yemen, al-Shabaab in Somalia and Boko Haram in Mali (Solomon 2014: n.p.). Administrative functions such as garbage collection and policing were performed by IS during the time they possessed the resources and capacity for them (Callimachi 2018a; Gerges 2016: 41; Mohamedou 2018: 109). It was a conscious arrangement, with IS establishing a hierarchical structure to govern and control the territory they occupied along with its inhabitants. Notwithstanding the international politics of state recognition, IS was engaged in the four activities of state making as organized violence identified by Tilly: war making, state making, protection and extraction (Tilly 1985: 181). Beyond the violence and focusing on the quotidian needs of everyday life, there were aspects of IS governance appreciated by those it governed, for example, the absence of bribery (Callimachi 2018a).

In 2018 *The New York Times* published two articles based on a large collection of IS documents gathered by its reporter (Callimachi 2018a, 2018b).[4] The specifics of life under IS governance reveal the extent to which they "monetized" the economy of the territory under control and the revenue generated as a result. Crucially, as noted in *The New York Times* article, everything was taxed, generating "hundreds of millions of dollars" just from the agricultural sector alone (Callimachi 2018b: D1). This reportage based on IS documents confirmed the earlier analysis made of IS financing and its sources. As explained in Chapter 2 in the discussion of FARC's operations in Colombia, controlling territory provides the insurgent/terrorist group with access to the resources of that territory. In other words, it possessed access to the agricultural and industrial production for tax purposes as well as the capacity to tax all trade and goods transiting the territory.[5] In this way the insurgent group is functioning like a state.

Fundraising like a state

As noted earlier, states generally finance themselves by exploiting the natural resources of their territory and by taxing the economic activity of the population of the territory. For IS oil was the source of income that received the most attention from 2014 as it gained control over oil fields in Syria and Iraq. In testimony to the US House of Representatives' Committee on Financial Services, Matthew Levitt stated that in August 2014 IS controlled approximately "350 oil wells in Iraq and 60% of Syria's oil fields" (Levitt 2014: 3). Production capacity at these well heads was not at its best and estimates for how much oil was produced under IS control varied. One article in August 2014 put production in the range of 30,000 to 70,000 barrels a day for that month, with production reported to have declined to 34,000 to 40,000 barrels a day in October 2015 (Malas & Abi-Habib 2014; Solomon, Chazan & Jones 2014). This decline in production was a product of airstrikes on production facilities and truck transport along with a reduced capacity to maintain and repair even those facilities that were not attacked.

Initially, airstrikes against oil infrastructure were limited, with the focus placed on preventing the passage of oil and oil products out of IS territory. In part this decision was taken to avoid civilian (non-IS) casualties among truck drivers and oil field workers. This choice also reflected a hope that the Syrian civil war would soon be resolved and the oil infrastructure and production capacity retained to finance a new Syrian government (Lubold & Dagher 2015). Moreover, the US government wanted to avoid any direct intervention in the Syrian conflict. As time passed this hope withered and died, and concern over the actions of IS to "cleanse" its territory increased (*The Economist* 2014). The air campaign that began in 2014 was expanded in late 2015 because the airstrikes over the previous year against oil infrastructure in IS territory had not reduced its ability to raise money as much as desired. A US government official was reported to say that IS continued to generate $500 million a year from oil production. Following IS's terrorist attacks in Paris in November 2015 the participation of French aircraft against IS increased and Russia also began attacking oil infrastructure in Syria (Solomon 2015b).

The air campaign against IS reduced oil production in the territory it controlled, with remaining capacity providing some revenue (Faucon & Coker 2016). In part this was because the group responded to the airstrikes by taking advantage of the concern of the US and its allies over inflicting collateral damage. Personnel and equipment identifiable as IS withdrew from proximity to the oil production facilities, leaving some traders buying oil confident that "smart bombs" were used. While IS vehicles were attacked, the nearby vehicles used by the local oil traders were not targeted (Solomon 2015b). Yet data on IS finances acquired during a raid in May 2015 that also led to the death of the group's finance chief revealed that its oil production peaked at 55,000 barrels a day in October 2014, several months after the air campaign began. Oil was continuing to contribute $46 million a month to the IS treasury (Faucon & Bradley 2015). The contribution of oil to its financing would continue in some form until IS forces were evicted from control of the territory with oil fields.

Another factor that influenced the role played by oil production in the financing of IS during the time it controlled territory was the global oil market. Local traders and businesses had little choice when purchasing oil products because of sanctions. But traders intending to export oil out of IS-controlled territory were competing with other sources of crude oil when attempting to resell it. Due to a massive increase in US oil production following the rise of fracking in 2014, global oil prices began to decline. From a peak of $112/barrel in June 2014, the global price of a barrel of oil was $61 in June 2015, $48 in June 2016 and $46 in June 2017.[6] Reports on IS oil production put its price in the range of $26/barrel to $35/barrel for heavy crude and $60/barrel for light crude in August 2014, when global oil prices were still near their peak (Malas & Abi-Habib 2014). Obviously, circumstances meant that IS had to sell its oil at a discounted price. In a *Financial Times* analysis last updated in February 2016, a table listing oil fields under IS control included their estimated production rate and price per barrel. It showed prices ranging from $20/barrel to $45/barrel, still discounted on global prices but not by as much as two years earlier. These prices reflected local conditions and continued local demand for petroleum products (Solomon, Kwong & Bernard 2016).[7]

While oil revenue as a source of funding for IS received much of the attention in the media and among analysts, taxing the economic activity of the population and territory under its control was equally important. In its study of the financing behind IS the FATF offered a short paragraph on "illicit taxation", referencing media reports of taxes imposed on all trade and the fees charged on the trucks that transported the goods (a road tax). The next paragraph in the FATF study highlighted a rather unexpected source of tax revenue, an "income tax" on the salaries of Iraqi civil servants in IS territory that continued to work for, and be paid by, the Iraqi government. The government stopped paying these salaries, along with the pensions that had been paid to retired staff, in July 2015 because IS was collecting anywhere from 10 to 50 per cent in tax from the recipients. With up to 400,000 civil servants in IS-controlled territory, the Iraqi government estimated that it had paid more than $1 billion in salaries before stopping this flow of money (Solomon & Jones 2015). Yet the situation had presented the Iraqi and US governments with a difficult dilemma to resolve as part of their campaign against IS. Continuing to pay salaries and pensions supported the civil servants and their families, yet it also gave IS a revenue stream to tax. The concern was that stopping this flow of money could result in a humanitarian crisis among those continuing to live under IS rule.

IS approached the task of governing territory with a plan, in a 24-page internal memorandum released sometime between July and October 2014 (Malik 2015b).[8] This document did not stand alone but built on an internal bureaucratic structure that developed as the group evolved and grew in the years before assuming control of territory in 2014 (al-Tamimi 2015). The work of administrating a bureaucracy and governing a territory requires a steady and consistent revenue stream. Oil revenues and income taxes from Iraqi civil servants initially provided a steady source, with data from one IS "province" showing the following breakdown for the month of January 2015: the revenue for that month was $8.4 million, with 44.7 per cent from confiscations, 27.7 per cent from oil and gas sales, 23.7 per cent from tax collections and 3.9 per cent from electricity usage (Malik 2015a). This may have been the peak of revenue collections for IS, yet as also noted in the article, even though this sum may look good for a terrorist group it was very meagre for a state. Later in 2015 revenue from oil sales and civil servant income taxes were reduced by the air campaign against oil infrastructure and the suspension of Iraqi government salaries and pensions. Moreover, confiscating property is a one-off source of revenue rather than a steady source of income. Consequently, IS's bureaucracy was forced to turn to other forms of taxation to make up the shortfall. Every step in farming, from purchasing seeds to selling the harvest, had a tax imposed on it, every merchant was taxed on the value of the goods to be sold, and every trader paid customs duties on the goods they brought into IS territory (Solomon & Jones 2015).

IS's taxation strategy extended beyond these transactions and included a wide variety of other activities as well. One that is not the normal practice of a state was the confiscation of property. The AML/CFT regime does encourage the confiscation of the illegal proceeds of crime because of its illegal origins and because crime should not pay (van Duyne, Harvey & Gelemerova 2018: 317–21).[9] IS, however, did not identify property for confiscation because of its illegal origins but because the property owner did not practice its form of Islam. Some groups could gain an exemption from this confiscation policy by paying *jizya*, a protection tax granting them permission to live within IS territory (Counter-Terrorism Committee Executive Directorate 2019: 23). Paying the tax, however, was not sufficient for protecting people, Iraqi and Syrian Christians for example, from the depredations of IS (Gerges 2016: 32–3). Other groups were not offered even this small reprieve. In 2014 IS took genocidal action against the Yazidi people, a minority religious group in the region. Beyond killing the Yazidis, driving survivors from their homes and destroying their religious and cultural sites, IS enslaved the women and girls (Gerges 2016: 30–32; Counter-Terrorism Committee Executive Directorate 2019: 21–6). To process the property and possessions confiscated from Yazidis, Christians and others, and then use it to generate income, IS established a Ministry of "War Spoils" (Callimachi 2018b). This ministry, in turn, sold the confiscated goods to other residents of the territory it controlled, and its fighters could purchase them at reduced prices (Solomon & Jones 2015).

Fundraising like an insurgent group

There are several fundraising methods used by IS in the same way that they have been used by other terrorist groups. These methods are in addition to those discussed in the previous section, which depended on controlling and governing territory. As explained previously, prior to 2014 the group funded itself with oil smuggling, extortion and trafficking in stolen merchandise, and IS continued to use these methods after losing control of territory. Their use of human trafficking by enslaving and selling Yazidis while controlling territory was touched on in the previous section. An investigation into the use of human trafficking for terrorist financing found that in addition to IS, it is also used by al-Shabab, Boko Haram and the Lord's Resistance Army. In addition to revenue, some of these groups have forced abducted individuals, often children, to serve the group as cooks, spies, messengers and combatants (Counter-Terrorism Committee Executive Directorate 2019: 28–9).[10]

A different perspective on the topic of human trafficking is found in the movement of individuals seeking to join IS. This phenomenon of foreign fighters, sympathetic non-combatants and family members attracted the attention of the UN along with the "sending" countries. The situation introduced another avenue of financing; the own resources brought by these IS "immigrants" and the remittances sent to them by family members at their request. The FATF report on the financing behind IS included discussions of foreign fighters bringing "material support" with them in the form of equipment and supplies, along with retaining access to their home bank accounts. Further, the foreign fighters received donations from friends and family, which were transferred to their bank account or sent directly to them in the conflict zone as a wire transfer or cash delivery. In one case from the UK, family members of a foreign fighter in Syria concealed the transfer of money by using a humanitarian aid convoy going to the region. They were subsequently convicted of terrorist financing, and unofficial aid convoys to the conflict zone ended (Casciani 2016). This case highlights a difficult problem with humanitarian aid to a conflict zone, separating legitimate aid from potential funding and material support for the groups involved in the conflict.

Over time some of the foreign fighters attracted to IS became disillusioned with the group as conditions changed when it lost control of territory in Iraq and Syria. The human trafficking networks that had been helping local civilians to escape IS control were now approached by foreign fighters also seeking to escape and return home. In other cases, captured foreign fighters were repatriated to their home country or traded/transferred to other insurgent groups (Solomon & Mhidi 2017a). Estimates for the total number of foreign fighters that succeeded in joining IS range from the 19,000 reported by the FATF in its report on IS (citing US government sources for the figure as of the end of 2014) up to a figure of 33,815 individuals identified in the dataset used in one academic analysis (Pokalova 2019: 800). The latter dataset, with its larger number of foreign fighters, found that they came from 103 different countries. The foreign fighters that remained with IS continue to be viewed as a threat to international peace and security by the UN, as will be discussed further.

Other measures to prevent money flowing to IS at the same time constrained the flow of financial aid to humanitarian groups operating in the area, along with the remittances sent to family and friends trapped under IS control. These measures constrained money intended for the internally displaced persons in refugee camps due to the worry that it could be redirected to IS members and supporters. This remains a concern as countries are forced to address the problem of captured IS fighters and their families. The ongoing conflict in Syria has forced people to remain in refugee camps, and humanitarian aid continues to be monitored to prevent it going to IS or any of the other internationally proscribed groups. Pivotal to the transfer of money to groups and individuals have been the exchange houses and other informal money service businesses operating on the periphery of IS territory. Frequently named as *hawala* (discussed in Chapter 3) in media reports, these businesses connect to exchange houses in the Persian Gulf states for transfers elsewhere in the world (Coker 2016). The US imposed financial sanctions on several it identified as supporting IS, but there was greater impact after the sanctions were also imposed by the other member states of its Terrorist Financing Targeting Center: Bahrain, Kuwait, Oman, Qatar, Saudi Arabia and the United Arab Emirates.[11]

Kidnapping for ransom is not unique to IS and has become a popular method by which to raise funds for a terrorist group operating in an insecure environment. The practice is also widely used by organized crime gangs in these insecure environments, leading to investigations on the existence of a nexus between organized crime and terrorism (Omelicheva & Markowitz 2021). In the case of IS one article described kidnapping for ransom as its "most widely reported enterprise", responsible for roughly $20 million in revenue in 2014 (Hansen-Lewis & Shapiro 2015: 145). The FATF investigation into IS finances indicated that hundreds of people had been kidnapped by the group, which generated ransom revenue in the range of $20 million to $45 million. It must be remembered that to pay a ransom to a terrorist group represents a violation of UN Security Council sanctions against that group. In the abstract this is a policy that everyone could agree with, up to the point at which the ransom is to recover someone that you care about, and then the policy doesn't matter and you just want that person back. In 2015 Japan was confronted with a demand for $200 million to ransom two Japanese citizens taken hostage by IS. The amount was determined by the sum of non-military aid that Japan had pledged in support of regional countries to help in their conflict with IS (Malik, McCurry & Chulov 2015). The ransom was not paid and subsequently IS released videos showing the beheading of both men (BBC News 2015).

A fundraising method that does appear to be specific to IS is the sale of historical artefacts and antiquities. On the one hand, trafficking in antiquities is no different from trafficking in any other illicit commodity, including untaxed cigarettes, cocaine, heroin and guns.[12] The opportunity for IS to profit from smuggling antiquities was due to their presence in the territory that IS controlled. Unfortunately there is a global demand for the private ownership of these historical artefacts, and IS simply assumed control over the existing smuggling networks and illegal digging. On the other hand, the fact that IS chose to continue the trade in antiquities is incongruous, given the publicity it sought through the destruction of museums and historical sites it deemed "unreligious" (Bailey 2015). Beyond collecting taxes from the diggers and smugglers already involved in the antiquities black market, IS actively promoted the practice. Investigations after IS had been expelled from Mosul and the surrounding area found that following its destruction of a shrine at Nabi Yunas in July 2014 further excavations took place in the hill beneath the remains of the shrine. Local residents informed the BBC team visiting the site in 2018 that IS hired local people to dig these tunnels and remove any portable artefacts the digging revealed. IS then sold them to the antiquities black market (Khoshnaw 2018).

While the black market in antiquities is not a new problem for law enforcement, the involvement of IS brought it to the attention of counterterrorism officials. The national apparatus to combat the financing of terrorism approached the black market trade in antiquities with a greater sense of urgency because it represented yet another way to neutralize IS. The FATF made several Recommendations in its report on IS finances specifically for dealing with the use of cultural artefacts by IS to raise revenue. These Recommendations began by providing a reminder that UN Security Council Resolution 2199 (2015) called on countries to prohibit the trade in black market antiquities. They continued by urging companies involved in the legitimate antiquities trade to establish policies requiring clear provenance on all items that they handle. Moreover, these companies were urged to report suspicious transactions and any item for sale that they knew to be stolen. As already required of the financial sector, the onus was placed on the antiquities sector to recognize and report any illicit actors and illicit activity to the proper authorities.

Media reports revealed the challenges involved with preventing the movement of black market antiquities in the auction rooms and store fronts of destination markets (Faucon & Kantchev 2017; Faucon, Kantchev & MacDonald 2017). It also must be recognized that at this point in the chain of transactions, IS has already collected its revenue from an earlier middleman. Confiscating the stolen antiquities from the end dealer or customer permits its repatriation to the country of origin but has not stopped or prevented terrorist financing. A statement by one expert emphasized the role of the demand for antiquities: "If no one was buying, people wouldn't dig it up" (Shabi 2015). Yet all the same, the demand for them preceded IS's involvement in the antiquities black market, and it continues to exist following IS's expulsion from the territory containing these archaeological sites. The problem is separate from and independent of terrorist financing. The actions of IS brought greater attention to it, but the remedy for the problem of black market antiquities is beyond the scope of this book (Russo & Giusti 2019). As was the case with oil as a source of IS financing, antiquities are no longer a revenue source now that the group no longer controls the territory within which they are found.

The trafficking in antiquities demonstrates once more that *any* economic transaction may be misused to finance terrorism. In 2021 the US government published draft rules for public comment that would place AML/CFT reporting requirements on dealers in the antiquities market (Tokar 2021). In part this action appears to be the result of court action in the US to recover antiquities that were "allegedly looted by Islamic State" in order to repatriate them to Iraq (Viswanatha & Kantchev 2017: n.p.).

The continuing threat of Islamic State

Defeat on the battlefield for IS, in terms of the loss of captured fighters and loss of control of territory, is not the same thing as defeating the group. As IS lost territory, it appears that the leadership sought to secure the future of the organization and retain as much of their accumulated financial assets as possible. Interviews with some of the people connected to exchange houses located outside of IS territory highlighted what they saw as a concerted effort by the group to shift money out of the region, with investment in Europe being one of the ultimate destinations. At the same time IS forced usage of its "domestic currency" of metal coinage in order for the group to accumulate the other currency (Syrian pounds, US dollars) in circulation for its own reserves (Solomon & Mhidi 2017b).[13] This strategy is consistent with what one author has identified as a "boom-bust" cycle of organizational existence among insurgent groups (Ahmad 2021). The logic derived from this study of jihadist groups is, in some ways, like the business cycle for an economic sector. When times are good the organization builds up its economic reserves, and these reserves in turn help the organization to survive the lean times of the "bust" phase of the cycle. Beyond its accumulated reserves, IS continued to extort "protection money" in those areas where it operates and collects profits from smuggling. Additionally, as mentioned in Chapter 6, the US Department of Justice seized cryptocurrency wallets connected with terrorist financing for IS. In that case, a businessman supporting the group set up a website in early 2020 taking advantage of the Covid-19 pandemic to sell fake personal protective equipment (Office of Public Affairs 2020).

The resumption of IS operating as an insurgent group seeking to undermine the authority and security of the recognized state in Iraq brought the fear that it also would undertake further terrorist attacks outside of the Middle East (Cornish & Khattab 2018). Accompanying this fear is a related concern over the captured foreign fighters that remain in refugee camps in Iraq. The UN reported that as they are released and return to their country of origin, the foreign fighters represent a source of continued radicalization if not properly rehabilitated and reintegrated into society (United Nations Secretary-General 2020: 3). At the same time, people that remain faithful to the aims of IS exercise influence and control in some parts of the refugee camps. In addition to maintaining discipline for faithfulness to IS policy, the adherents collect a percentage of remittances sent to the residents of the camps as revenue to support IS (Coles & Faucon 2021).

Contrary to some assessments, the financing that supported IS after 2014 was "exceptional" only in the fact that the group controlled territory from which it could extract revenue. It is true that some of its forms of extraction, such as the confiscation of property and imposition of slavery, were more brutal than the methods used by other insurgent groups. But the fundamental reason for the size of its treasury remains the fact that in the Weberian sense it was a state. IS, for a period of time, exercised the monopoly of violence over the population of the territory that it controlled. And prior to 2014 it already possessed substantial capital that it was able to build up in the anarchic environment that was Iraq and Syria in those years. Regardless of the various estimates for the amount of money collected and possessed by IS, at the time that it controlled territory those sums were not sufficient for the task of providing public services. As noted in one news article, if IS had been recognized as a state, "it would be a country of the poor" (Solomon 2015a: n.p.). At the same time, conventional CFT methods, as introduced with al Qaida, operate within the international financial system. Because IS was less reliant on foreign donations and cross-border transfers those methods had less impact against it.

The circumstances in Iraq and Syria represented a dilemma for many of the countries concerned by its potential to increase transnational terrorism. Confrontation of a terrorist group that was in control of territory occupied by an unwilling population meant there were constraints on possible courses of action. The situation was recognized and acknowledged in August 2014 as IS was extending its control of territory across Iraq:

> "Can you prevent ISIS from taking assets? Not really, because they're sitting on a lot of assets already," said a Western counterterrorism official. "So you must disrupt the network of trade. But if you disrupt trade in commodities like food, for example, then you risk starving thousands of civilians." (Malas & Abi-Habib 2014: n.p.)

But this situation does not mean that standard measures to combat the financing of terrorism were not attempted. The UN Security Council added to its sanctions list the names of individuals accused of supporting and financing IS following the group's expansion and control of territory in 2014:

> The U.N. sanctions were the first international effort to stem the groups' revenues and operations. But counterterrorism experts said that,

because so much of the revenue is domestic and other trade is done in
a cash-only region, there are few effective ways to clamp down.

(Malas & Abi-Habib 2014: n.p.)

More aggressive measures could have created undesirable consequences for the
local population living under IS control, potentially leading to a larger humanitarian crisis in the region.

The experience of applying the global regime to counter money laundering
and terrorist financing against IS exposed gaps in its methods and practices
when dealing with a group controlling territory. The historical experience with
other cases, including FARC and LTTE, predated the introduction of terrorist
financing as a concern for global governance in 2001. Consequently only AML
measures were used in those cases, and they lacked the additional capabilities
that were introduced with the combatting of terrorist financing, such as the
consolidated list of sanctions maintained by the UN Security Council. Moreover,
imposing limits on the transfer of money into the region surrounding IS's zone of
control impacted more than just the group. It also affected the flow of humanitarian aid and migrant remittances (Daher 2020). The action taken to enforce
measures to combat the financing of terrorism imposed these unintended
consequences on non-combatants, with the potential to undermine the legitimacy of this global governance regime.

8

REFLECTIONS ON COMBATTING TERRORIST FINANCING

Our understanding of terrorist financing has changed over the past 70 years and that evolution of terrorist financing was presented across Chapters 1–4. In addition, to place the parallel development of measures to combat the financing of terrorism in context, the introduction of money laundering as a crime was discussed, along with the establishment of the FATF. An international organization, the FATF was created to understand money laundering and it first produced guidance to help countries combat money laundering in 1990. In 2001 the organization's mandate was expanded to include terrorist financing, making the FATF the responsible organization for producing international guidance to combat terrorist financing as well. The historical development of both terrorist financing and the regime to counter it provided the background for understanding the contemporary issues impacting the CFT regime that were explored in Chapters 5–7.

There are several key points to take away from this book regarding the measures used to combat the financing of terrorism. First, there was the initial focus placed on terrorist financing by the US government in 2001. As shown, their claim that terrorist financing is the "lifeblood" of terrorism was a justification for pre-emptive sanctions. The lifeblood image, however, is a flawed analogy. It implied that it would be possible to prevent future acts of terrorism by freezing assets, preventing fundraising and stopping the transfer of money. The diverse set of terrorist attacks in Europe between 2001 and 2021 demonstrate that this is not the case. In those attacks the perpetrators variously used their own salaries and savings, took out small bank loans, engaged in petty crime and received contributions from foreign terrorist groups. The CFT measures operating in Europe did not provide advance warning of any of these attacks. Rather, the information gathered by these measures came into use only after the fact to trace the source of financing behind the attack. Following the attacks in Paris in November 2015, for example, the French government identified the use of anonymous prepaid cards by the terrorists and introduced a proposal to regulate them in the future.

The second point to recall is that freezing the known assets of a terrorist group had limited impact. Before acting to freeze someone's assets and prevent their use to support terrorism it was necessary to identify the assets belonging to the known terrorist. Yet anyone that was only suspected of a connection with a known terrorist also had their assets frozen. This approach implicated innocent bystanders alongside known terrorist financiers. To pre-emptively freeze the assets of a potential supporter of terrorism introduced a human rights dimension to CFT actions. This human rights dimension should be situated alongside the apparent ineffectiveness of asset freezing to prevent terrorist financing. To think of the process this way reveals the fact that asset freezes operate differently for CFT purposes than in their use as part of the targeted sanctions imposed on a head of state and their associates. To apply financial sanctions in a terrorist financing case the process often targeted individuals with few assets, and they were frequently based on little publicly available evidence connecting this person to terrorism. Moreover, the total amount of terrorist assets frozen worldwide is substantially less than the sums that have been attributed to grand corruption (e.g. the case of Ferdinand Marcos, see Chaikin & Sharman 2009). Consequently, the application of asset freezing as a tool to prevent terrorist finance was of limited use following the initial set of UN Security Council sanctions imposed in 2001.

Another point to recall is that there are two dimensions to the processes employed to combat the financing of terrorism. The first dimension consists of those processes used to identify the fundraising mechanisms of a terrorist group and taking action to interdict their misuse by the group. The second dimension involves the CFT measures interdicting the transfer of funds to the terrorist group. Different methods are employed to deal with each dimension. The fundraising dimension initially placed attention on the use of charities by al Qaida to raise funds from sympathizers, and later on the use of black market antiquities by IS. The funds transfer dimension brought to the attention of government officials *hawala* and other informal value transfer systems used to make cross-border transfers without the reporting requirements imposed on the financial sector. As new payment methods were developed using technological advancements, such as the internet and mobile phones, it was necessary to introduce new measures designed to prevent their misuse for terrorist financing. Efforts to prevent the misuse of any payment method to support terrorist financing will experience variable success. The central feature to recognize here is that the evolution of CFT measures reinforces the fact that any economic transaction creating revenue can be used as terrorist financing. Yet whatever the method employed, there is always a point where it is preferred to have the revenue as money, as this is widely accepted and largely anonymous.

The role of money for CFT

To place the global regime against money laundering and terrorist financing into context, the opening chapter provided a brief discussion of the nature of money. The economic actions performed by notes and coins have increasingly moved to credit/debit cards, mobile money and digital currencies. The use of the latter forms of payment to facilitate terrorist financing was explored in Chapter 5. Also explored were some of the measures employed to prevent the misuse of these payment methods in all forms of criminality. The guidance created to prevent the misuse of new payment methods for terrorist finance continues to be the same guidance issued for AML laws. The debate over the usefulness of this "follow the money" strategy continues today. In 2001 William Wechsler argued that following the money would provide the means to deal with money laundering by "drug cartels, arms traffickers, terrorist groups, and common criminal organizations" (Wechsler 2001: 40). This former US Treasury official emphasized the ease of international banking services created by globalization that, in turn, enabled tax evasion as well as money laundering. Recognize, however, that his analysis was published before CFT measures were introduced by the FATF in October 2001 and before the UN Convention for the Suppression of the Financing of Terrorism went into force in April 2002 after its ratification by 22 countries. In early 2001 his policy concern was that the new George W. Bush administration would backtrack on the efforts to strengthen international cooperation against money laundering and tax evasion achieved by the Clinton administration (Wechsler 2001: 55–7). This concern proved ephemeral following the terrorist attacks in the US. The policy recommendations offered in his article for strengthening US and international efforts against money laundering and terrorist financing were included in the wide ranging USA PATRIOT Act (2001).

The proposition that following the money helped to combat terrorist financing remained contested and was revisited in 2017 in the same American journal that published Wechsler (2001). In the later analysis, however, Peter Neumann sought to make the case that the methods employed in the international CFT regime did not work and that "the war on terrorist financing has failed" as a result (Neumann 2017a: 93). While acknowledging the CFT campaign "has probably deterred terrorists from using the international financial system", Neumann then pointed out that there is no evidence that CFT measures have prevented an act of terrorism (Neumann 2017a: 94).

He proceeded to specify some of the problems created by the international regime. They include bank derisking activity along with the essential problem of preventing the possible misuse of any economic transaction as a source of terrorist financing. One example for this concern was the alleged use of the illegal ivory trade by al Shabab in East Africa (Neumann 2017a: 97). Further examples Neumann listed as representing the failure of the present system include IS, which did not use the international financial system that is the focus of the FATF Recommendations. Beyond their failure to stop IS there is the fact that self-funded attacks by individuals or small groups also have not been exposed by monitoring bank accounts. Neumann's overarching conclusion, therefore, is that the present CFT approach is not working and it needs to be "tailored to the group" and their methods of financing rather than seeking a global one-size-fits-all strategy (Neumann 2017a: 102).

Rebuttals to Neumann's critique were published two issues later by several advocates of the methods and practices employed by the current international regime for combatting terrorist finance. One of these short pieces included several brief references to terrorist attacks that were apparently prevented by the lack of funds, as well as the August 2006 bomb plot in the UK that allegedly was exposed by financial data (Levitt & Baurer 2017). Both authors formerly served in US Treasury Department offices responsible for dealing with terrorist financing, so consequently their reference to these examples may be due to personal knowledge of non-public data. Yet a news article reviewing the 2008 trial of those arrested for the aforementioned UK bomb plot did not include money or financing in the list of evidence presented to the jury (Sciolino 2008). A second rebuttal defending the current regime against terrorist financing emphasized the role that financial sanctions performed in discouraging potential donors from supporting a terrorist group. It further noted the involvement of non-financial private companies such as auction houses to counter IS's smuggling networks. These private companies also began to submit suspicious transaction reports about antiquities for sale (Lindholm & Realuyo 2017). Given that the smuggling networks pre-existed IS, the attention given to the black market in illegal antiquities should help to protect this cultural heritage (Singh 2017: 635–7). The involvement of dealers and auction houses at the end node of the smuggling network, however, did little to prevent IS from raising revenue at the beginning of the network (as explained in Chapter 7). Neumann's reply to these rebuttals re-emphasized his point that they offered no evidence to support the efficacy of current CFT practices. Moreover, they provided "no systematic data" to demonstrate "the effectiveness of the current approach" and justify the current methods and techniques used against terrorist financing (Neumann 2017b: 149).

The question of efficacy

Revisiting the debate on the efficacy of the international regime against terrorist financing in the pages of "the leading forum for serious discussion of American foreign policy and global affairs"[1] (*Foreign Affairs* magazine) reminds us of the continuing tension in the US over its twenty-first-century "global war on terror". The US-based debate continues in its failure to address the intended and unintended consequences that plague the rest of the world from the ongoing campaign against transnational terrorism. In some ways Neumann's critique of CFT practices are equally applicable to the global regime against money laundering. Many of the problems seen with AML enforcement are the same as those affecting CFT. The significant difference between the two objectives rests with the urgency behind CFT, as the potential terrorist attack represents a threat to national security. The 2021 conviction of NatWest bank "for breaching anti-money laundering regulations" may have been the first for a bank in the UK under its AML laws (Croft & Venkataramakrishnan 2021). Yet the case also highlighted a number of ways in which the entire AML edifice is unstable. An April 2021 article in *The Economist* used this case to open its analysis and make the argument that "the war against money-laundering is being lost". This article declared that the problem was, in part, due to the fact that the AML regime has "major structural flaws" (*The Economist* 2021). The large compliance sector that has grown to implement the finance industry's AML obligations had achieved some successes. Yet this article cited several analyses reporting that little criminal money was confiscated as a result of that success and carried echoes of an earlier article in *The Economist*, published in 2005, on the regime established against terrorist finance. The earlier article noted that four years after terrorist financing was placed on the international agenda the compliance costs to implement CFT in the financial sector had soared. Yet for all the money spent these compliance measures had "yielded depressingly few tangible results", and the article observed that the terrorist attacks experienced in 2005 "often seem to involve very little money" (*The Economist* 2005: n.p.).

One solution proposed to address the efficacy issue is to improve the extent and effectiveness of public–private cooperation. Some commentators suggest that cooperation, or *improved* cooperation, between regulatory authorities (financial intelligence units – FIUs) and financial institutions (their compliance staff) would lead to better AML/CFT enforcement (Keatinge & Keen 2020). The suggestion that increased cooperation is all that is required is somewhat forgetful of the forced nature of private sector cooperation. Clearly compliance staff are patriotic citizens concerned about stopping terrorism, yet their jobs exist as a result of this privatization of security. Moreover, the objective of the compliance role is more about complying with relevant laws and regulations than it is about exposing terrorist financiers (Tsingou 2018). Evidence presented at the NatWest trial, for example, demonstrated that frontline employees followed their training and reported the suspicious transactions internally. The issue exposed by this case was that the "quality and adequacy" of internal bank processes were not sufficient for the task of preventing money laundering at NatWest (Croft & Venkataramakrishnan 2021). In other words, compliance procedures beyond these customer-facing staff failed to process the suspicious transaction reports up the line and on to regulators.

Improved cooperation in the form of "public–private partnerships" was one of several points raised by the FATF Executive Secretary at a conference in March 2021:

> The authorities need to give banks more specific information and the intelligence required to find real suspicious activity and to focus their huge investment and resources on activity that makes a difference. We need to break down the barriers to more effective information sharing, including the myths and realities that remain around tipping off and data protection. (Lewis 2021: n.p.)

Buried in these two sentences is the central challenge for a liberal, democratic society: the balance between liberty and security (Waldron 2003). The report in *The Economist* on the current state of the international AML regime described data privacy laws as "a daunting obstacle" for information exchange. It was one of the "three big problems" identified as limiting the "fight against financial crime" (*The Economist* 2021: 62–3). What appears to be forgotten in the account offered in *The Economist* and its concern with fighting global financial crime is that this obstacle consists of the same data privacy laws that are intended to protect the individual. Information gathering by large corporations, and in particular during 2021 the data collected and used by social media companies, received a lot of attention. In turn, this attention encouraged legislatures to propose new laws to increase the protection of personal privacy.[2]

Central to addressing the efficacy of the global regime created to stop terrorist financing are two questions. First, to what extent must the economy be constrained in pursuit of this goal? And second, how much should we be prepared to pay for this goal? These questions concern the size of the compliance industry and the cost of maintaining it, which is placed on customers, shareholders and society at large. The argument made by Neumann (2017a) is that the current approach does not actually work at preventing terrorist finance. It is not, in other words, efficacious, or perhaps it is simply that the costs outweigh the benefits (Pol 2020). Beyond the cost of compliance for firms there are further costs to society, some of which may not be measurable. These costs arise from the unintended consequences created by an international regime that seeks to exclude from the global financial system those individuals and groups that want to finance terrorism. Yet simultaneously they are excluding the people that governments want included in the formal financial system for the benefits it would bring to national economic development.

Mitigating unintended consequences

The debate over the efficacy of AML/CFT practices, procedures and laws is often focused on their ability to satisfy the main goal: to stop money laundering and prevent the financing of terrorism. The justification behind the creation of the Financial Action Task Force was to assess the extent of international cooperation to prevent money laundering and to develop additional methods for preventing it. For the first years of its existence the FATF operated under a periodically renewed temporary mandate. This mandate was initially established by the G7 in 1989, and in 2019 the G7 announced that from 2020 the FATF would have an open-ended mandate. This announcement made the FATF a permanent international club of select member states and territories. As discussed throughout the previous chapters the Forty Recommendations of the FATF possess a number of unintended consequences. Chief among them is the "know your customer" obligation that operates as a barrier to financial inclusion for those people unable to provide the necessary identity documents. In recent years the FATF has become more receptive towards some of the criticism directed at it regarding the unintended consequences of its actions and directives. A RUSI study sponsored by the Bill and Melinda Gates Foundation in 2020 explored some of the concerns and the study summarized the financial inclusion barrier in a succinct sentence: "Those who already contend with physical, educational and cultural barriers to accessing finance can struggle the most to meet the financial crime requirements that stem from the FATF system" (Chase, van der Valk & Keatinge 2021: ix).

The FATF initiated a project in February 2021 to investigate the concerns raised over unintended consequences and to collect suggestions for resolving and avoiding them in the future. Yet interestingly the FATF framed the existence of unintended consequences in its statement as the result of "the incorrect implementation of the FATF Standards". The organization apparently does not recognize the possibility that the deficiency may be with the Forty Recommendations themselves. For example, the emphasis in the Forty Recommendations on formal economy businesses and financial institutions with little recognition for the conduct of informal economies throughout the world. Another example for an unintended consequence is the use of AML laws to address a different set of government concerns. An investigative report published by Reuters highlighted the use of AML laws to suppress NGOs, political opponents and government critics in India, Serbia and Uganda (Berwick 2021). Further commentary from the experts at RUSI's Centre for Financial Crime and Security Studies pointed out that there is no penalty for countries that *intentionally* misuse their AML legislation in this way. Specifically it highlighted the use of AML laws by countries to constrain the operation of foreign-funded NGOs (Keatinge, Reimer & Chase 2021).[3]

In October 2021 the FATF released its first public document from their project investigating unintended consequences. The short document provided a "High-Level Synopsis of the Stocktake" conducted to investigate ways of mitigating the problem of unintended consequences.[4] It specifically covered bank derisking, financial exclusion, targeting NGOs and the "curtailment of human rights". The Synopsis concluded that the FATF has been "actively responding" to the identified unintended consequences for a number of years. The next phase of the project seeks to examine how the issues identified may be addressed, including possible revisions to existing FATF guidance.

For the FATF the limited success of the CFT regime to prevent terrorism does not lie with the Forty Recommendations. Instead it is fundamentally a failure by governments to adequately perform the risk analysis necessary to implement the risk-based approach promulgated in its guidance. Yet the situation remains that the private sector firm is concerned with avoiding censure, fines and criminal convictions, while the government seeks to avoid getting the country placed on the FATF "grey list" because of its negative economic impact. Consequently these states seek to perform well enough to be considered compliant the next time they undergo an FATF mutual evaluation assessment (Berwick 2021). In addition to the efforts of the FATF and the FSRBs to improve AML/CFT methods and techniques over the past three decades, criminals and terrorists have also changed their practices to avoid exposure and arrest. The extension of the Forty Recommendations beyond its initial focus on banking to other economic sectors reflects the innovations taken by criminals to launder their money. And the use of new payment methods such as prepaid debit cards reflects innovations taken by terrorists as well as money launderers, leading to their inclusion in FATF reports and standards (Keatinge & Danner 2021).

The future for interdicting terrorist finance

The global regime to combat the financing of terrorism is but one part of the larger effort to address transnational terrorism. A crucial aspect that seems underappreciated when considering the efficacy of the campaign against terrorist finance is the underlying *political* motivations behind the use of violence as a substitute for electoral politics. This means that it is important to look beyond the question of efficacy and the trade-off between costs and benefits in a financial war on terrorism. The earlier mentioned debate rehearsed in the pages of *Foreign Affairs* made little mention of the politics that drive individuals and groups to use acts of terrorism to draw attention to their cause. Similarly, the FATF's "High-Level Synopsis" made no reference to the political motivations behind terrorist financing. When analysing the regime to combat the financing of terrorism we should remain conscious of the political motivations behind the actions of the people that are choosing to finance acts of terrorism.

For scholars and students studying the international regime to combat the financing of terrorism there are several areas that deserve further attention. The lack of "systematic data" identified by Neumann (2017b: 149) is a problem that should be explored. The challenge with undertaking this research is the fact that the information available may be limited if the researcher is not granted access to the data collected by government agencies. As noted previously, the unintended consequences should not only be identified, but practicable remedies that may be implemented in a low-capacity country found. Such remedies would support financial inclusion and further economic development. In parallel, while the FATF and its member states may feel these unintended consequences are the result of the incorrect application of the guidance, an alternate understanding should be explored. It would involve research in low-capacity countries to investigate ways to implement regulations that address AML/CFT concerns while operating in an economy with a large informal sector. In other words, to identify practices and procedures that do not rely on the privatization of security to achieve success in the continuing effort to prevent the financing of terrorism.

NOTES

1 Foundations and origins

1. The full text of the treaty, in English, is available at https://www.un.org/law/cod/finterr. htm (accessed 6 May 2021). The webpage for the treaty's entry in the United Nations Treaty Collection is https://treaties.un.org/pages/ViewDetails.aspx?src=TREATY&mtdsg _no=XVIII-11&chapter=18&clang=_en (accessed 6 May 2021), and this page includes the list of signatory states.
2. There are alternate terms and acronyms, for example "counter-terrorist financing (CTF)" is used by some commentators (e.g. Ryder 2015). This book will use CFT throughout, reflecting its use by the FATF and UN, and their prominent role in promulgating international policy against terrorist financing.
3. For a preview, see the US State Department website, https://www.state.gov/state-spons ors-of-terrorism/ (accessed 10 May 2021).
4. The FATF highlights this point in the history of its first 30 years with the story of Pablo Escobar and a photo of the gate at his Colombian estate, which had the plane he first used to transport cocaine to the US on top, see "Financial Action Task Force – 30 years", https:// www.fatf-gafi.org/publications/fatfgeneral/documents/fatf-30.html (accessed 10 May 2020).
5. The full text of the treaty, in English, is available at https://www.unodc.org/unodc/en/treat ies/illicit-trafficking.html (accessed 6 April 2022).
6. For example, by the UN Office on Drugs and Crime, https://www.unodc.org/unodc/en/ money-laundering/overview.html, and the FATF, http://www.fatf-gafi.org/faq/moneylau ndering/.
7. Money laundering can be seen as an element in a number of films over the years, including *Bad Boys II* (2003), *Sicario* (2015) and *The Accountant* (2016).
8. The reports are available on the FATF website, http://www.fatf-gafi.org/publications/ methodsandtrends/ (accessed 12 May 2021).
9. See https://www.fatf-gafi.org/about/membersandobservers/ (accessed 21 May 2021).

2 Terrorist financing in the twentieth century

1. This report reprints the December 1993 issue of *Fire Engineering* magazine; the initial article, with colour images, is available online at https://www.fireengineering.com/leaders hip/the-bombing-of-the-world-trade-center/ (accessed 27 May 2021).
2. These were not the first international agreements to address political violence; a collection published in 1979 contains a set of documents, treaties and resolutions beginning with the 1902 "Treaty for the Extradition of Criminals and for Protection Against Anarchism", signed in Mexico City (Alexander, Browne & Nanes 1979).

3. Event data on terrorist attacks are available online at the Global Terrorism Database, maintained by the National Consortium for the Study of Terrorism and Responses to Terrorism, which is resident at the University of Maryland (https://www.start.umd.edu/gtd/, accessed 31 May 2021); and the RAND Database of Worldwide Terrorism Incidents, which covers the period 1968–2009 (https://www.rand.org/nsrd/projects/terrorism-incidents.html, accessed 31 May 2021).

4. See https://www.state.gov/state-sponsors-of-terrorism/ (accessed 31 May 2021).

5. An online archive version of the report, "Patterns of Global Terrorism, 1990", is maintained by the Federation of American Scientists at https://fas.org/irp/threat/terror_90/index.html (accessed 31 May 2021).

6. See the CoE website, https://www.coe.int/en/web/portal/home (accessed 4 June 2021).

7. This work is organized under the Committee of Experts on the Evaluation of Anti-Money Laundering Measures and the Financing of Terrorism (MONEYVAL), https://www.coe.int/en/web/moneyval/home (accessed 4 June 2021).

8. For a list of these transnational terrorists see the appendix for Nesser (2015), "Chronology of Jihadism in Europe 1994–2015", which is available online at https://www.hurstpublishers.com/wp-content/uploads/2015/11/Islamist-Terrorism-in-Europe-Appendix.pdf (accessed 24 May 2021).

9. Nesser states the terrorist cell involved was more transnational than previous Islamist groups in Europe. For the plot against the Strasbourg Christmas Market in France, the group was based in Germany while the plan was conceived of in Afghanistan and supported by individuals based in the UK (Nesser 2015: 95).

10. See Prevention of Terrorism (Temporary Provisions) Act 1989, Schedule 1, Proscribed Organisations, https://www.legislation.gov.uk/ukpga/1989/4/contents/enacted (accessed 7 June 2021).

11. The term "political violence" is used at this point to underscore the political agenda behind the group labeled as "terrorist" by the government in power. Such a terrorist group may be pursuing self-determination, the overthrow of the government or re-unification, as in the case of the IRA.

12. This point was made by the former British Prime Minister Sir Edward Heath during the Q&A session following his public lecture at Ohio University when the author was an undergraduate student.

13. It is interesting to observe that Ross (1991) makes no mention of contributions from Irish diasporas, even though it was recognized as a problem and this legal Note was published in the *Boston College International and Comparative Law Review*.

14. For example, the edited collection *Terrorism Financing and State Responses: A Comparative Perspective* does not include the case of the UK and the financing behind the IRA, nor is the IRA mentioned in the chapter on "Terrorism Financing in Europe" (Napoleoni 2007). In total there are four page references for Irish Republican Army in the index of the book (Giraldo & Trinkunas 2007b: 361).

15. See https://www.state.gov/foreign-terrorist-organizations/ (accessed 9 June 2021).

3 In the aftermath of 9/11

1. This Executive Order is available on the US State Department website, https://www.state.gov/executive-order-13224/ (accessed 15 June 2021).

2. See https://www.govinfo.gov/app/details/PLAW-107publ56/summary (accessed 16 June 2021).

3. Though not all were unfamiliar. As reported by John Berlau, one person was quite knowledgeable on *hawala* and sought to focus US government attention on it in 1999 (Berlau

2003). *Hawala* and other forms of informal value transfer are discussed in the section "Spreading the net".

4. See the "1996–1997 Report on Money Laundering Typologies", available at http://www. apgml.org/fatf-and-fsrb/documents/default.aspx?s=title&c=5433ad41-3c44-4a43-86a2-256b5ad23720&pcPage=2 (accessed 17 June 2021).

5. See https://www.fincen.gov/money-services-business-definition (accessed 18 June 2021).

6. See https://www.fatf-gafi.org/glossary/j-m/ (accessed 18 June 2021). The FATF definition also includes a reference to "new payment methods", which are discussed further in Chapter 6.

7. The Commission's website is archived at https://www.9-11commission.gov/ (accessed 18 June 2021).

8. See the interpretive note for Recommendation 8 of the FATF's "Forty Recommendations".

9. It is worth noting that the implementation of AML/CFT reporting obligations in the legal profession varies among countries, even between the EU and the US; see Nougayrede (2019).

10. Regulation (EC) No. 1781/2006 on information on the payer accompanying transfers of funds.

11. Regulation (EC) No. 1889/2005 on controls of cash entering or leaving the community.

12. For the current status of the EU's measures against terrorist financing, see https://ec.eur opa.eu/home-affairs/what-we-do/policies/counter-terrorism/fight-financing-terrorism_ en (accessed 9 September 2021).

13. See https://eur-lex.europa.eu/eli/dir/2018/1673/oj (accessed 22 June 2021).

14. See https://www.unodc.org/unodc/en/treaties/illicit-trafficking.html (accessed 22 June 2021).

15. This is the illegal activity that produced the money that needs to be laundered.

16. The Financial Crimes Enforcement Network (FinCEN) maintains an online tool for accessing SAR statistics at https://www.fincen.gov/reports/sar-stats (accessed 23 June 2021).

17. There is a further financial sector that received public exposure in the 2008 financial crisis: shadow banking. These non-financial firms are not licensed as banks but they were lending money to other businesses. The size and role of some of these so-called "shadow banks" was pivotal in the financial unwinding that occurred in 2008–09 (Pozsar *et al.* 2013).

18. At about the same time the World Bank initiated its work on remittances (World Bank 2003).

19. See https://www.swift.com/ (accessed 25 June 2021).

20. See also, "Terrorist Finance Tracking Program", https://www.swift.com/about-us/legal/ compliance-0/terrorist-finance-tracking-program (accessed 15 July 2021), and "Data Protection Policies", https://www.swift.com/about-us/legal/compliance/data-protection-policies/frequently-asked-questions (accessed 15 July 2021).

21. See https://ec.europa.eu/info/law/law-topic/data-protection_en (accessed 16 July 2021).

22. See https://www.pclob.gov/ (accessed 16 July 2021).

4 Collective action against terrorist financing

1. The 1267 Committee is currently known as the "ISIL (Da'esh) & Al-Qaida Sanctions Committee", with information at https://www.un.org/securitycouncil/sanctions/1267 (accessed 29 July 2021).

2. The nature of the EU as a level of governance operating between the UN Security Council at a global level and the level of individual states (including the European states that are also members of the Security Council) may be one reason for the level of academic interest.

3. See https://www.un.org/securitycouncil/ombudsperson (accessed 3 August 2021).

4. Moreover, it should be noted that the introduction of due process through the role of the Ombudsperson operates solely for targeted sanctions to prevent terrorist financing. The other targeted sanctions regimes of the Security Council do not include a process of challenge and review (Prost 2018: 918).
5. The current list can be found at https://www.un.org/securitycouncil/sanctions/1267/aq_sanctions_list/summaries (accessed 4 August 2021), under the Committee's webpage at https://www.un.org/securitycouncil/sanctions/1267 (accessed 4 August 2021).
6. See also de Londras (2019: 230–35).
7. See https://undocs.org/A/RES/60/288 (accessed 10 August 2021).
8. See https://www.un.org/counterterrorism/ (accessed 10 August 2021).

5 Making CFT global

1. There is also a discussion of "illicit financial flows" involving developing economies that, in some instances, incorporates terrorist financing alongside money laundering. This aspect of illicit financial flows is not addressed here, and one starting point for the literature on it is Kahler *et al.* (2018).
2. It is also important to recognize that the law is socially constructed, such that in some national societies prostitution and recreational drug use are not illegal. Increasingly among US states, for example, marijuana use is being decriminalized, reflecting a shift in the social construction of marijuana as a dangerous product and situating it as more comparable to alcohol and tobacco.
3. The Aadhaar system is not without problems, see the BBC News article at https://www.bbc.com/news/world-asia-india-43207964 (accessed 9 May 2018).
4. See http://www.fatf-gafi.org/topics/fatfrecommendations/documents/rba-and-de-risking.html (accessed 6 April 2022).
5. See the statement at https://www.fatf-gafi.org/publications/high-risk-and-other-monitored-jurisdictions/documents/call-for-action-june-2021.html (accessed 19 July 2021). For the FATF's current list of "High-risk and other monitored jurisdictions" see https://www.fatf-gafi.org/publications/high-risk-and-other-monitored-jurisdictions/documents/call-for-action-february-2020.html (accessed 19 July 2021).
6. See, for example, the experience of BNP Paribas SA, which was fined $8.97 billion by the US government for violating US sanctions against Cuba, Iran and Sudan over the period 2002–12 (Barrett, Matthews & Johnson 2014).
7. The ESAAMLG region comprises 18 member states, see https://www.esaamlg.org/index.php/countries (accessed 7 September 2021).
8. See https://www.fatf-gafi.org/publications/fatfgeneral/documents/outcomes-fatf-plenary-june-2021.html (6 April 2022) and https://www.fatf-gafi.org/publications/financialinclusionandnpoissues/documents/unintended-consequences-project.html (accessed 3 September 2021).
9. Syria was under US sanctions because it was listed as a state-sponsor of terrorism; see Chapter 2 for the discussion of state-sponsored terrorism.
10. See http://www.fatf-gafi.org/publications/fatfgeneral/documents/outcomes-plenary-october-2016.html (accessed 6 April 2022).
11. Which is not to say that other countries are not concerned about terrorist financing taking place in Brazil. In December 2021 the US Treasury identified a "network of al-Qaʼida-affiliated individuals and their companies" in Brazil as terrorist financiers now under US financial sanctions (US Treasury 2021).
12. The discussion of the situation in West Africa, however, did include a brief update on Boko Haram (Analytical Support and Sanctions Monitoring Team 2021b: 7).

6 Dealing with new payment technologies

1. Available from the Asia/Pacific Group on Money Laundering at http://www.apgml. org/includes/handlers/get-document.ashx?d=da10600f-0fb4-4ece-9c1c-c69376c870c5 (accessed 17 June 2021).
2. For Apple Pay see https://www.apple.com/apple-pay/ (accessed 23 September 2021), and for Google Pay see https://safety.google/pay/ (accessed 23 September 2021).
3. Using a cheque or money order to place the initial value on the prepaid card, rather than cash, did require the presentation of ID documents, effectively starting a CDD process.
4. For more information on ACH see https://www.nacha.org/ (accessed 24 September 2021); on SEPA see https://www.ecb.europa.eu/paym/integration/retail/sepa/html/index.en.html (accessed 24 September 2021); and on SWIFT see https://www.swift.com/ (accessed 24 September 2021).
5. See https://www.gsma.com/ (accessed 24 September 2021).
6. Registration of mobile phone SIMs was introduced to counter the use of disposable, unregistered phones ("burner phones") for illicit activity (Theodorou 2013: 10).
7. Terrorist financing was not mentioned in the indictment, see https://www.justice.gov/arch ive/criminal/ceos/pressreleases/downloads/DC%20egold%20indictment.pdf (accessed 1 October 2021).
8. Zetter (2009) observes that this perception about the applicability of CDD regulations was held by many of the early internet payment service companies.
9. See https://about.pypl.com/who-we-are/history-and-facts/default.aspx (accessed 30 September 2021).
10. See https://www.paypal.com/uk/smarthelp/article/faq1253 (accessed 4 October 2021).
11. See https://www.paypal.com/us/smarthelp/article/why-do-i-have-to-confirm-my-identity-to-hold-a-balance-with-paypal-faq3834, https://www.paypal.com/us/smarthelp/article/faq1758 and https://www.paypal.com/us/smarthelp/article/faq734 (all accessed 1 October 2021). These PayPal FAQ pages are for the US and the information and requirements for other countries may be different.
12. This can be found on the US government website, available at https://www.ussc.gov/sites/default/files/pdf/training/annual-national-training-seminar/2018/Emerging_Tech_Bit coin_Crypto.pdf (accessed 14 June 2022).
13. Current valuations of different cryptocurrencies are available online at several websites, e.g. https://www.coinbase.com/price (accessed 6 October 2021).
14. See https://www.fatf-gafi.org/publications/virtualassets/documents/virtual-assets.html (accessed 6 October 2021).
15. In 2019 Europol announced the "First law enforcement action of its kind against such a cryptocurrency mixer service", see https://www.europol.europa.eu/newsroom/news/multi-million-euro-cryptocurrency-laundering-service-bestmixerio-taken-down (accessed 13 October 2021).
16. See https://www.elliptic.co/ (accessed 7 October 2021).
17. See https://www.diem.com/en-us/ (accessed 6 January 2021).

7 The financing of Islamic State

1. See the table at Mohamedou (2018: 90) for a chronology of the evolution of IS and its leadership.
2. At the time of writing a story has emerged of workmen involved in the reconstruction of Mosul who discovered bags of currency in the underground vaults of the Central Bank branch (AFP 2021).

3. See "Financing of the Terrorist Organisation Islamic State in Iraq and the Levant (ISIL)".
4. The removal of the documents from Iraq by this reporter raised concerns for the Middle East Studies Association's Committee on Academic Freedom, see https://mesana.org/advocacy/committee-on-academic-freedom/2018/05/02/acquisition-and-unethical-use-of-documents-removed-from-iraq-by-rukmini-callimachi (accessed 20 October 2021). The documents are now stored at George Washington University, to be digitized and made available online at https://isisfiles.gwu.edu/?locale=en (accessed 20 October 2021). This instance was not, however, the first case of reporting on IS involving documents removed from Iraq. A report in the *The Wall Street Journal* in 2016 used documents seized and removed by the US military in a raid, see Faucon and Coker (2016).
5. Imposing taxes on goods in transit, particularly opium, also financed the Taliban in Afghanistan, see *The Economist* (2019).
6. Historical data on oil prices is available from the US Energy Information Administration at https://www.eia.gov/dnav/pet/pet_pri_spt_s1_d.htm (accessed 27 October 2021).
7. This investigative report is available at https://ig.ft.com/sites/2015/isis-oil/ (accessed 28 October 2021).
8. An English translation of the document is available at *The Guardian* newspaper website, https://www.theguardian.com/world/2015/dec/07/islamic-state-document-masterplan-for-power (accessed 2 November 2021).
9. Clearly stated in Recommendation 4, "Confiscation and provisional measures", of the Forty Recommendations.
10. The use of child soldiers by insurgent groups is a problem separate from terrorist financing and addressed in a diverse literature, see Fox (2021).
11. See also the US Treasury Department press release, https://home.treasury.gov/news/press-releases/sm1057 (accessed 15 November 2021).
12. This discussion benefits from the research assistance of Colleen A. M. Gargiulo in support of my contribution to the jointly authored paper, "Cultural Genocide and Terrorism Financing: ISIS and the Erasure of History", with Jorge Lasmar and Rashmi Singh, which was presented at the International Studies Association Conference, San Francisco, on 7 April 2018.
13. For more on the establishment of an IS currency, see Oxnevad (2016).

8 Reflections on combatting terrorist financing

1. As described on its webpage, https://www.foreignaffairs.com/about-foreign-affairs (accessed 13 December 2021).
2. *The Wall Street Journal*, for example, published a series of articles under the heading of "The Facebook Files" based on a trove of Facebook's internal company documents, see https://www.wsj.com/articles/the-facebook-files-11631713039 (accessed 31 December 2021).
3. Just as there are multiple reasons for a financial firm to reduce its risk, AML/CFT legislation is not the only way to constrain the foreign funding of NGOs. India, for example, has a Foreign Contribution Regulation Act that has been in force since 1976 and that is designed to limit the use of foreign funds to finance domestic political groups (Das 2021).
4. See https://www.fatf-gafi.org/publications/financialinclusionandnpoissues/documents/unintended-consequences-project.html (accessed 23 December 2021).

REFERENCES

The documents of the Financial Action Task Force are available on their website, https://www.fatf-gafi.org/publications/ (accessed 6 April 2022). The Resolutions of the United Nations Security Council are available on their website, https://www.un.org/securitycouncil/content/resolutions-0 (accessed 6 April 2022).

AFP 2021. "Iraq finds water-logged cash in Mosul central bank coffers". France24, 20 October. https://www.france24.com/en/live-news/20211020-iraq-finds-water-logged-cash-in-mosul-central-bank-coffers (accessed 25 October 2021).

Ahmad, A. 2021. "The long jihad: the boom-bust cycle behind jihadist durability". *Journal of Global Security Studies* 6(4): 1–17. doi: 10.1093/jogss/ogaa048.

Ahmad, A., C. Green & F. Jiang 2020. "Mobile money, financial inclusion and development: a review with reference to African experience". *Journal of Economic Surveys* 34(4): 753–92. doi: 10.1111/joes.12372.

Al-Salhy, S. & T. Arango 2014. "Sunni militants drive Iraqi army from big city: assault on Mosul puts region at risk of war". *The New York Times*, 11 June.

al-Tamimi, A. 2015. "The evolution in Islamic State administration: the documentary evidence". *Perspectives on Terrorism* 9(4): 117–29.

Alexander, Y., M. Browne & A. Nanes (eds) 1979. *Control of Terrorism: International Documents*. New York, NY: Crane, Russack.

Alldridge, P. 2003. *Money Laundering Law: Forfeiture, Confiscation, Civil Recovery, Criminal Laundering and Taxation of the Proceeds of Crime*. Oxford: Hart.

Amicelle, A. 2011. "The great (data) bank robbery: terrorist finance tracking program and the 'SWIFT Affair'". Paris: Centre d'études et de recherches internationales, Sciences Po.

Amicelle, A. & E. Jacobsen 2016. "The cross-colonization of finance and security through lists: banking policing in the UK and India". *Environment and Planning D: Society and Space* 34(1): 89–106.

Analytical Support and Sanctions Monitoring Team 2007. "Sixth Report, S/2007/132". United Nations Security Council. Last modified 8 March. https://www.un.org/securitycouncil/sanctions/1267/monitoring-team/reports (accessed 14 June 2022).

Analytical Support and Sanctions Monitoring Team 2009. "Tenth Report, S/2009/502". United Nations Security Council. Last modified 2 October. https://www.undocs.org/S/2009/502 (accessed 12 August 2011).

Analytical Support and Sanctions Monitoring Team 2021a. "Twenty-seventh Report, S/2021/68". United Nations Security Council. Last modified 3 February. https://www.undocs.org/S/2021/68 (accessed 7 July 2021).

Analytical Support and Sanctions Monitoring Team 2021b. "Twenty-seventh Report, S/2021/655". United Nations Security Council. Last modified 15 July. https://www.undocs.org/S/2021/655 (accessed 4 August 2021).

Arnold, M. 2020. "Germans dash for cash despite virus transmission worries". *Financial Times*, 25 March.

Associated Press 2006. "EU bankers say they had no power to block secret SWIFT bank data transfer deal with U.S". *International Herald Tribune*, 4 October.

Azinge, N. 2019. "A regulatory misfit? A closer look at the counter-terrorist financing strategies in African states". *Journal of Banking Regulation* 20(3): 245–59. doi: 10.1057/s41261-018-0087-y.

Bailey, D. 2015. "Palmyra: Islamic State's demolition in the desert". BBC News, 5 October. https://www.bbc.co.uk/news/world-middle-east-34294287 (accessed 20 October 2021).

Bangasser, P. 2000. *The ILO and the Informal Sector: An Institutional History*. Geneva: International Labour Organization.

Bank for International Settlements 2020. *Annual Economic Report*. Basel: Bank for International Settlements.

Barrett, D., C. Matthews & A. Johnson 2014. "BNP Paribas draws record fine for 'Tour de Fraud'". *The Wall Street Journal*, 30 June. http://online.wsj.com/articles/bnp-agrees-to-pay-over-8-8-billion-to-settle-sanctions-probe-1404160117 (accessed 5 July 2014).

Barry, R. & R. Ensign 2016. "Losing count: U.S. terror rules drive money underground". *The Wall Street Journal*, 30 March. http://www.wsj.com/articles/losing-count-u-s-terror-rules-drive-money-underground-1459349211 (accessed 31 March 2016).

Bazarbash, M. *et al.* 2020. "Mobile money in the COVID-19 pandemic". Washington, DC: International Monetary Fund.

BBC News 2015. "Japan outraged at IS 'beheading' of hostage Kenji Goto". BBC News, 1 February. https://www.bbc.co.uk/news/world-middle-east-31075769 (accessed 12 November 2021).

Berlau, J. 2003. "Show us your money". Reason, November, 22–29.

Berwick, A. 2021. "Special report: how a little-known G7 task force unwittingly helps governments target critics". Reuters, 5 August. https://www.reuters.com/business/fina nce/how-little-known-g7-task-force-unwittingly-helps-governments-target-critics-2021-08-05/ (accessed 28 December 2021).

Bhatia, M. (ed.) 2008. *Terrorism and the Politics of Naming*. Abingdon: Routledge.

Biersteker, T. & S. Eckert 2008. "Introduction: the challenge of terrorist financing". In T. Biersteker & S. Eckert (eds), *Countering the Financing of Terrorism*, 1–16. London: Routledge.

Biersteker, T., S. Eckert & P. Romaniuk 2008. "International initiatives to combat the financing of terrorism". In T. Biersteker & S. Eckert (eds), *Countering the Financing of Terrorism*, 234–59. London: Routledge.

Biersteker, T., M. Tourinho & S. Eckert 2016. "Thinking about United Nations targeted sanctions". In T. Biersteker, S. Eckert & M. Tourinho (eds), *Targeted Sanctions: The Impacts and Effectiveness of United Nations Action*, 11–37. Cambridge: Cambridge University Press.

Bilefsky, D. 2006. "European lawmakers criticize Swift and ECB on bank data". *International Herald Tribune*, 4 October.

Board of Governors of the Federal Reserve System *et al.* 2005. Joint Statement on Providing Banking Services to Money Services Businesses. Washington, DC. https://www.fincen.gov/resources/statutes-regulations/guidance/joint-statement-providing-banking-servi ces-money-services (accessed 7 August 2021).

Brummer, C. 2012. *Soft Law and the Global Financial System: Rule Making in the 21st Century*. Cambridge: Cambridge University Press.

Bureau of Counterterrorism 2020. "Country reports on terrorism 2019". US Department of State. https://www.state.gov/reports/country-reports-on-terrorism-2019/ (accessed 9 June 2021).

Bureau of Diplomatic Security 2019. "1993 World Trade Center Bombing". US Department of State, 21 February. https://www.state.gov/1993-world-trade-center-bombing/ (accessed 9 June 2021).

Bush, George W. 2001. "President Freezes Terrorists' Assets". Washington, DC, Office of the Press Secretary, last revised 24 September, available at http://georgewbush-whitehouse. archives.gov/news/releases/2001/09/20010924-4.html (accessed 18 April 2012).

Byman, D. 2005. *Deadly Connections: States that Sponsor Terrorism*. Cambridge: Cambridge University Press.

Callimachi, R. 2018a. "In ISIS territory, justice was swift for petty beefs". *The New York Times*, 2 July.

Callimachi, R. 2018b. "The ISIS files". *The New York Times*, 8 April.

Campbell-Verduyn, M. 2018. "Bitcoin, crypto-coins, and global anti-money laundering governance". *Crime, Law and Social Change* 69(2): 283–305. doi: 10.1007/s10611-017-9756-5.

Carlisle, D. 2019. "Countering the use of cryptocurrencies for terrorist financing". Elliptic blog, 10 February. https://www.elliptic.co/blog/countering-terrorist-financing-cryptocurrency (accessed 10 February 2021).

Casciani, D. 2016. "Syria aid convoys: two guilty over terror funding". BBC News, 23 December. http://www.bbc.com/news/uk-38419488 (accessed 1 January 2017).

Cassara, J. 2015. *Trade-Based Money Laundering: The Next Frontier in International Money Laundering Enforcement*. Hoboken, NJ: Wiley.

Cassella, S. 2002. "Forfeiture of terrorist assets under the USA PATRIOT Act of 2001". *Law and Policy in International Business* 34: 7–16.

Chadha, V. 2015. *Lifeblood of Terrorism: Countering Terrorism Finance*. New Delhi: Bloomsbury Publishing India.

Chaikin, D. 2009. "How effective are suspicious transaction reporting systems?" *Journal of Money Laundering Control* 12(3): 238–53.

Chaikin, D. & J. Sharman 2009. *Corruption and Money Laundering: A Symbiotic Relationship*. Basingstoke: Palgrave Macmillan.

Charities Commission for England and Wales 2016. Chapter 2: Due diligence, monitoring and verifying the end use of charitable funds. Charities Commission for England and Wales. https://www.gov.uk/government/collections/protecting-charities-from-harm-complia nce-toolkit (accessed 14 July 2021).

Chase, I., J. van der Valk & T. Keatinge 2021. "Assessing the Financial Action Task Force's impact on digital financial inclusion". RUSI Occasional Papers. London: Royal United Services Institute.

Chernick, M. 2007. "FARC-EP: from liberal guerillas to Marxist rebels to post-Cold War insurgents". In M. Heiberg, B. O'Leary & J. Tirman (eds), *Terror, Insurgency and the State: Ending Protracted Conflicts*, 51–81. Philadelphia, PA: University of Pennsylvania Press.

Chulov, M. 2014. "How an arrest in Iraq revealed Isis's $2bn jihadist network". *The Guardian*, 15 June. https://www.theguardian.com/world/2014/jun/15/iraq-isis-arrest-jihadists-wea lth-power (accessed on 19 October 2021).

Clunan, A. 2006. "The fight against terrorist financing". *Political Science Quarterly* 121(4): 569–96.

Cochrane, F. 2007. "Irish-America, the end of the IRA's armed struggle and the utility of 'soft power'". *Journal of Peace Research* 44(2): 215–31. doi: 10.1177/0022343307075123.

Coker, M. 2016. "How Islamic State's secret banking network prospers". *The Wall Street Journal*, 24 February. http://www.wsj.com/articles/how-islamic-states-secret-banking-network-prospers-1456332138 (accessed on 25 February 2016).

Coles, I. & B. Faucon 2021. "Refugee camp for families of Islamic State fighters nourishes insurgency". *The Wall Street Journal*, 9 June. https://www.wsj.com/articles/refugee-camp-for-families-of-islamic-state-fighters-nourishes-insurgency-11623254778 (accessed 12 June 2021).

Committee on Appropriations 1999. Counterterrorism and Infrastructure Protection. Prepared statement of Louis J. Freeh. Washington, DC: US Government Printing Office, last revised 4 February. https://www.govinfo.gov/app/details/CHRG-106shrg57802/CHRG-106shrg57 802 (accessed 27 May 2021).

Cooper, B. *et al.* 2020. *De-risking and illicit financial flows: the role of regional economic hubs.* South Africa: Cenfri. https://cenfri.org/publications/derisking-illicit-financial-flows-regio nal-economic-hubs-africa/ (accessed 26 December 2020).

Cordes, B. *et al.* 1984. "Trends in international terrorism, 1982 and 1983". Document no. R-3183-SL. Santa Monica, CA: Rand Corporation. https://www.rand.org/pubs/reports/R3183.html (accessed 31 May 2021).

Cornish, C. & A. Khattab 2018. "Isis returns to insurgent roots after battlefield defeats". *Financial Times*, 5 December.

Council of Europe 1980. "Measures against the transfer and safekeeping of funds of criminal origin: recommendation and explanatory memorandum". In Rec(80)10E. https://search.coe.int/cm/Pages/result_details.aspx?ObjectID=09000016804f6231 (accessed 7 June 2005).

Counter-Terrorism Committee Executive Directorate 2019. *Identifying and Exploring the Nexus Between Human Trafficking, Terrorism, and Terrorism Financing.* New York, NY: United Nations Security Council.

Cramér, P. 2003. "Recent Swedish experiences with targeted UN sanctions: the erosion of trust in the Security Council". In E. de Wet, A. Nollkaemper & P. Dijkstra (eds), *Review of the Security Council by Member States*, 85–106. Antwerp: Intersentia.

Croft, J. & S. Venkataramakrishnan 2021. "NatWest's anti-money laundering failures laid bare in gold dealer case". *Financial Times*, 16 December.

Daher, J. 2020. *Invisible Sanctions: How Over-compliance Limits Humanitarian Work on Syria.* Berlin: IMPACT, Civil Society Research and Development.

Daragahi, B. 2014. "Biggest bank robbery that 'never happened' – $400m Isis heist". *Financial Times*, 17 July.

Das, A. 2021. "India's strict rules on foreign aid snarl Covid donations". *The New York Times*, 12 May.

de Goede, M. 2003. "Hawala discourse and the war on terrorist finance". *Environment and Planning D* 21(5): 513–32.

de Goede, M. 2005. "Risk and the war on terrorist finance". *Operational Risk*, March, 36–41.

de Goede, M. 2011. "The SWIFT affair and the global politics of European security". *Journal of Common Market Studies* 50(2): 214–30.

de Goede, M. & M. Wesseling 2017. "Secrecy and security in transatlantic terrorism finance tracking". *Journal of European Integration* 39(3): 253–69. doi: 10.1080/07036337.2016.1263624.

de Koker, L. & N. Jentzsch 2013. "Financial inclusion and financial integrity: aligned incentives?" *World Development* 44: 267–80.

de Londras, F. 2019. "The transnational counter-terrorism order: a problématique". *Current Legal Problems* 72(1): 203–51. doi:10.1093/clp/cuz005.

de Oliveira, I. 2018. "The governance of the financial action task force: an analysis of power and influence throughout the years". *Crime, Law and Social Change* 69(2): 153–72. doi:10.1007/s10611-017-9749-4.

Demirgüç-Kunt, A. *et al.* 2018. *The Global Findex Database 2017: Measuring Financial Inclusion and the Fintech Revolution.* Washington, DC: International Bank for Reconstruction and Development/The World Bank.

Dodd, N. 2014. *The Social Life of Money.* Princeton, NJ: Princeton University Press.

Doherty, B. 2021. "The alt-currency martyr". Reason, April, 20–28.

Eckert, S. 2008. "The US regulatory approach to terrorist financing". In T. Biersteker & S. Eckert (eds), *Countering the Financing of Terrorism*, 209–33. London: Routledge.

Eckert, S., T. Biersteker & M. Tourinho (eds) 2016. "Introduction". In Targeted Sanctions, 1–10.

The Economist 2005. "Looking in the wrong places: financing terrorism". *The Economist*, 22 October, 73–5.

The Economist 2014. "Mission relaunched: America and Islamic State". *The Economist*, 27 September.

The Economist 2019. "State departure: why Afghanistan's government is losing the war with the Taliban". *The Economist*, 18 May.

The Economist 2021. "Losing the war". *The Economist*, 17 April, 62–3.

El Taraboulsi-McCarthy, S. 2018. "The challenge of informality: counter-terrorism, bank de-risking and financial access for humanitarian organisations in Somalia". HPG working paper, Overseas Development Institute.

El Taraboulsi-McCarthy, S. & C. Cimatti 2018. "Counter-terrorism, de-risking and the humanitarian response in Yemen: a call for action". HPG working paper, Overseas Development Institute.

Engelmann, L. 1979. *Intemperance: The Lost War Against Liquor*. New York, NY: The Free Press.

English, R. 2009. *Terrorism: How to Respond*. Oxford: Oxford University Press.

English, R. 2016. "The future study of terrorism". *European Journal of International Security* 1(2): 135–49. doi:10.1017/eis.2016.6.

Ensign, R. 2015. "PayPal to pay $7.7 million to U.S. over alleged sanctions violations". *The Wall Street Journal*, 25 March. http://www.wsj.com/articles/paypal-to-pay-7-7-million-to-u-s-over-alleged-sanctions-violations-1427312161 (accessed 27 March 2015).

European Commission 2008. "Commission Regulation (EC) No 1190/2008 of 28 November 2008 amending for the 101st time Council Regulation (EC) No 881/2002 imposing certain specific restrictive measures directed against certain persons and entities associated with Usama bin Laden, the Al-Qaida network and the Taliban". *Official Journal of the European Union* L series 322: 25–6. Strasbourg.

European Commission 2019. "Commission Staff Working Document". SWD (2019) 301 final. Brussels.

European Court of Justice 2008. "Judgment of the Court (Grand Chamber) in the Joined cases C-402/05 P and C-415/05 P". Eur-Lex, 3 September. https://eur-lex.europa.eu/legal-content/EN/TXT/?uri=CELEX:62005CJ0402 (accessed 3 August 2021).

Faucon, B. & M. Bradley 2015. "After Paris attacks, air campaign escalates against Islamic State oil assets". *The Wall Street Journal*, 30 November. http://www.wsj.com/articles/after-paris-attacks-air-campaign-escalates-against-islamic-state-oil-assets-1448894011 (accessed 5 December 2015).

Faucon, B. & M. Coker 2016. "The rise and deadly fall of Islamic State's oil tycoon". *The Wall Street Journal*, 24 April. http://www.wsj.com/articles/the-rise-and-deadly-fall-of-islamic-states-oil-tycoon-1461522313 (accessed 25 April 2016).

Faucon, B. & G. Kantchev 2017. "Prominent art family entangled in ISIS antiquities-looting investigations". *The Wall Street Journal*, 31 May. https://www.wsj.com/articles/prominent-art-family-entangled-in-investigations-of-looted-antiquities-1496246740 (accessed 2 June 2017).

Faucon, B., G. Kantchev & A. MacDonald 2017. "The men who trade ISIS loot". *The Wall Street Journal*, 6 August. https://www.wsj.com/articles/the-men-who-trade-isis-loot-150 2017200 (accessed 7 August 2017).

Financial Conduct Authority (FCA) 2018. *Financial Crime: Analysis of Firms' Data*. London: Financial Conduct Authority.

Financial Crimes Enforcement Network 2014. *FinCEN Statement on Providing Banking Services to Money Services Businesses*. Washington, DC: US Department of the Treasury.

Flood, Z. 2013. "Barclays set to exit remittance business". *Financial Times*, 4 July, Beyond BRICS.

Fox, M. 2021. "Child soldiers research: the next necessary steps". *Small Wars & Insurgencies* 32(6): 1–11. doi:10.1080/09592318.2021.1990489.

Ganguly, M. 2001. "A banking system built for terrorism". *Time*, 5 October.

Gehring, T. & T. Dörfler 2013. "Division of labor and rule-based decisionmaking within the UN Security Council: the Al-Qaeda/Taliban sanctions regime". *Global Governance* 19(4): 567–87. doi:10.1163/19426720-01904006.

Gehring, T., C. Dorsch & T. Dörfler 2019. "Precedent and doctrine in organisational decision-making: the power of informal institutional rules in the United Nations Security Council's activities on terrorism". *Journal of International Relations and Development* 22(1): 107–35. doi:10.1057/s41268-017-0101-5.

General Court of the European Union 2010. "The General Court annuls the regulation freezing Yassin Abdullah Kadi's funds". Curia. https://ec.europa.eu/commission/presscorner/detail/en/CJE_10_95 (accessed 30 July 2021).

Gerges, F. 2016. *ISIS: A History*. Princeton, NJ: Princeton University Press.

Gilmore, W. 2011. *Dirty Money: The Evolution of International Measures to Counter Money Laundering and the Financing of Terrorism*. Fourth edn. Strasbourg: Council of Europe Publishing.

Giraldo, J. & H. Trinkunas 2007a. "The political economy of terrorism financing". In J. Giraldo & H. Trinkunas (eds), *Terrorism Financing and State Responses: A Comparative Perspective*, 7–20. Stanford, CA: Stanford University Press.

Giraldo, J. & H. Trinkunas 2007b. *Terrorism Financing and State Responses: A Comparative Perspective*. Stanford, CA: Stanford University Press.

González Zarandona, J., C. Albarrán-Torres & B. Isakhan 2018. "Digitally mediated iconoclasm: the Islamic State and the war on cultural heritage". *International Journal of Heritage Studies* 24(6): 649–71. doi:10.1080/13527258.2017.1413675.

The Guardian 2003. "Four convicted of Strasbourg bomb plot". *The Guardian*, 10 March. https://www.theguardian.com/world/2003/mar/10/germany.france (accessed 25 May 2021).

The Guardian 2021. "Met police seize nearly £180m of bitcoin in money laundering investigation". *The Guardian*, 13 July. https://www.theguardian.com/technology/2021/jul/13/met-police-bitcoin-money-laundering-cryptocurrency (accessed 14 July 2021).

Hameiri, S. & L. Jones 2016. "Global governance as state transformation". *Political Studies* 64(4): 793–810. doi:10.1111/1467-9248.12225.

Hansen-Lewis, J. & J. Shapiro 2015. "Understanding the Daesh economy". *Perspectives on Terrorism* 9(4): 142–55.

Harris, P., B. Wazir & K. Connolly 2002. "Al-Qaeda's bombers used Britain to plot slaughter". *The Observer*, 21 April. https://www.theguardian.com/world/2002/apr/21/terrorism.religion (accessed 25 May 2021).

Hayes, B. 2012. "Counter-terrorism, 'policy laundering' and the FATF: legalising surveillance, regulating civil society". Transnational Institute and Statewatch.

Horwitz, J. & P. Olson 2019. "Facebook unveils cryptocurrency Libra in bid to reshape finance". *The Wall Street Journal*, 18 June. https://www.wsj.com/articles/facebook-unveils-crypto-wallet-based-on-currency-libra-11560850141 (accessed 23 June 2019).

Houben, R. & A. Snyers 2020. *Crypto-assets: Key Developments, Regulatory Concerns and Responses*. Luxembourg: Committee on Economic and Monetary Affairs.

Hülsse, R. 2008. "Even clubs can't do without legitimacy: why the anti-money laundering blacklist was suspended". *Regulation & Governance* 2(4): 459–79. doi:10.1111/j.1748-5991.2008.00046.x.

Ingham, G. 1996. "Money is a social relation". *Review of Social Economy* 54(4): 507–29.

Ingham, G. 2004. *The Nature of Money*. Cambridge: Polity.

International Labour Organization (ILO) 2012. "Statistical update on employment in the informal economy". Geneva: International Labour Organization (ILO) Department of Statistics.

International Monetary Fund 2019. "US$100 bill on the rise". IMF Blog, 8 November. https://blogs.imf.org/2019/07/25/us100-bill-on-the-rise/ (accessed 8 November 2019).

Jackson, E. 2004. *The PayPal Wars: Battles with eBay, the Media, the Mafia, and the Rest of Planet Earth*. Los Angeles, CA: World Ahead Publishing.

Johnston, R. & I. Carrington 2006. "Protecting the financial system from abuse: challenges to banks in implementing AML/CFT standards". *Journal of Money Laundering Control* 9(1): 48–61.

Jupp, J. & M. Garrod 2019. "Legacies of the troubles: the links between organized crime and terrorism in Northern Ireland". *Studies in Conflict & Terrorism* Early view: 1–40. doi:10.1080/1057610X.2019.1678878.

Jusi, I., A. Satrya & B. Wardoyo 2019. "Terrorist financing through the internet in Indonesia: methods and vulnerabilities". Third International Conference on Strategic and Global Studies, Sari Pacific, Jakarta, Indonesia.

Kahler, M. *et al.* 2018. *Global Governance to Combat Illicit Financial Flows: Measurement, Evaluation, Innovation.* New York, NY: Council on Foreign Relations.

Kaufman, M. 2001. "Somalis said to feel impact of US freeze of al-Barakaat". *The Washington Post*, 30 November.

Keatinge, T. & F. Keen 2017a. "Humanitarian action and non-state armed groups: the impact of banking restrictions on UK NGOs". Chatham House Humanitarian Engagement with Non-state Armed Groups. London: Royal Institute of International Affairs.

Keatinge, T. & F. Keen 2017b. "Lone-actor and small cell terrorist attacks: a new front in counter-terrorist finance?" RUSI Occasional Papers. London: Royal United Services Institute.

Keatinge, T. & F. Keen 2020. "A sharper image advancing a risk-based response to terrorist financing". RUSI Occasional Papers. London: Royal United Services Institute.

Keatinge, T. & K. Danner 2021. "Assessing innovation in terrorist financing". *Studies in Conflict & Terrorism* 44(6): 455–72. doi:10.1080/1057610X.2018.1559516.

Keatinge, T., S. Reimer & I. Chase 2021. "Good intentions: The FATF faces its own unintended consequences". RUSI Commentary. London: Royal United Services Institute, last revised 5 August. https://rusi.org/explore-our-research/publications/commentary/good-intenti ons-fatf-faces-its-own-unintended-consequences (accessed 13 August 2021).

Kharif, O. 2020. "Facebook-backed Libra Association changes its name to Diem". Bloomberg, 1 December. https://www.bloomberg.com/news/articles/2020-12-01/facebook-backed-crypto-group-libra-changes-name-to-diem-network (accessed 6 January 2021).

Khoshnaw, N. 2018. "Explore the IS tunnels: how the Islamic State group destroyed a mosque but revealed a 3,000-year old palace". BBC News, 22 November. https://www.bbc.co.uk/news/resources/idt-sh/isis_tunnels (accessed 1 January 2019).

Kipkemboi, K., J. Woodsome & M. Pisa 2019. "Overcoming the Know Your Customer hurdle: innovative solutions for the mobile money sector". London: GSM Association.

Klein, A. 2020. "Statement by Chairman Adam Klein on the Terrorist Finance Tracking Program". Washington, DC: Privacy and Civil Liberties Oversight Board.

KPMG International 2004. "Global Anti-Money Laundering Survey 2004: how banks are facing up to the challenge". KPMG International.

KPMG International 2014. "Global Anti-Money Laundering Survey 2014". KPMG International.

Laqueur, W. 1986. "Reflections on terrorism". *Foreign Affairs* 65(1): 86–100. doi: 10.2307/20042863.

Lasmar, J. 2019. "When the shoe doesn't fit: Brazilian approaches to terrorism and counter-terrorism in the post-9/11 era". In M. Boyle (ed.), *Non-Western Responses to Terrorism*, 221–45. Manchester: Manchester University Press.

Leuprecht, C. *et al.* 2019. "Tracking transnational terrorist resourcing nodes and networks". *Florida State University Law Review* 46(2): 289–344.

Levey, S. 2006. "Statement on the Terrorist Finance Tracking Program". Office of Public Affairs. Last modified 23 June. https://home.treasury.gov/news/press-releases/js4334 (last accessed 15 June 2022).

Levitt, M. 2014. *Terrorist Financing and the Islamic State.* Washington, DC: Washington Institute for Near East Policy.

Levitt, M. & K. Baurer 2017. "Bank on it". *Foreign Affairs* 96(6): 144–6.

Lewis, D. 2021. "Speech at the Chatham House Illicit Financial Flows Conference". Financial Action Task Force. https://www.fatf-gafi.org/publications/fatfgeneral/documents/chat ham-house-march-2021.html (accessed 13 August 2021).

Libra Association 2019. Libra White Paper. Geneva: Libra Association.

Libra Association 2020. Libra White Paper v2.0. Geneva: Diem Association.

Lichtblau, E. 2003. "US wants foreign leaders' laundered assets". *The New York Times*, 23 August. https://www.nytimes.com/2003/08/23/us/us-wants-foreign-leaders-laundered-assets.html (accessed 15 June 2022).

Lichtblau, E. & J. Risen 2006. "Bank data sifted in secret by US to block terror". *The New York Times*, 23 June. http://www.nytimes.com/2006/06/23/washington/23intel.html (accessed 23 June 2006).

Lindholm, D. & C. Realuyo 2017. "Money talks". *Foreign Affairs* 96(6): 146–8.

Lubold, G. & S. Dagher 2015. "US airstrikes target Islamic State oil assets". *The Wall Street Journal*, 16 November. http://www.wsj.com/articles/french-airstrikes-in-syria-may-have-missed-islamic-state-1447685772 (accessed 16 November 2015).

Lyon, D. 2003. *Surveillance after September 11*. Cambridge: Polity.

Malas, N. & M. Abi-Habib 2014. "Islamic State economy runs on extortion, oil piracy in Syria, Iraq". *The Wall Street Journal*, 28 August. http://online.wsj.com/articles/islamic-state-fills-coffers-from-illicit-economy-in-syria-iraq-1409175458 (accessed 31 August 2014).

Malik, S. 2015a. "The Isis papers: behind 'death cult' image lies a methodical bureaucracy". *The Guardian*, 7 December. https://www.theguardian.com/world/2015/dec/07/isis-papers-guardian-syria-iraq-bureaucracy (accessed 2 November 2021).

Malik, S. 2015b. "The Isis papers: leaked documents show how Isis is building its state". *The Guardian*, 7 December. https://www.theguardian.com/world/2015/dec/07/leaked-isis-document-reveals-plan-building-state-syria (accessed 2 November 2021).

Malik, S., J. McCurry & M. Chulov 2015. "Islamic State video threatens lives of two Japanese hostages". *The Guardian*, 20 January. https://www.theguardian.com/world/2015/jan/20/islamic-state-video-japanese-hostages-jihadi-john (accessed 12 November 2021).

Martin, A. 2021. "Aadhaar in a box? Legitimizing digital identity in times of crisis". *Surveillance & Society* 19(1): 104–08.

Maurer, B. 2012. "Mobile money: communication, consumption and change in the payments space". *Journal of Development Studies* 48(5): 589–604. doi: 10.1080/00220388.2011.621944.

McCoy, T. 2014. "ISIS just stole $425 million, Iraqi governor says, and became the 'world's richest terrorist group' ". *The Washington Post*, 12 June. https://www.washingtonpost.com/news/morning-mix/wp/2014/06/12/isis-just-stole-425-million-and-became-the-worlds-richest-terrorist-group/ (accessed 25 October 2021).

McCullagh, D. 2004. "PayPal settles over gambling transfers". CNET.com. https://www.cnet.com/news/paypal-settles-over-gambling-transfers/ (accessed 4 October 2021).

Medd, R. & F. Goldstein 1997. "International terrorism on the eve of a new millennium". *Studies in Conflict & Terrorism* 20(3): 281–316. doi:10.1080/10576109708436040.

Medina, L. & F. Schneider 2018. *Shadow Economies Around the World: What Did We Learn Over the Last 20 Years?* Washington, DC: International Monetary Fund.

Milton-Edwards, B. 2017. "Securitizing charity: the case of Palestinian zakat committees". *Global Change, Peace & Security* 29(2): 161–77. doi:10.1080/14781158.2017.1302415.

Minnella, C. 2019. "Counter-terrorism resolutions and listing of terrorists and their organizations by the United Nations". In E. Shor & S. Hoadley (eds), *International Human Rights and Counter-Terrorism*, 31–53. Singapore: Springer.

Mitsilegas, V. 2014. "Transatlantic counterterrorism cooperation and European values: the elusive quest for coherence". In D. Curtin & E. Fahey (eds), *A Transatlantic Community of Law: Legal Perspectives on the Relationship between the EU and US Legal Orders*, 289–315. Cambridge: Cambridge University Press.

Moghadam, A. 2012. "Failure and disengagement in the Red Army Faction". *Studies in Conflict & Terrorism* 35(2): 156–81. doi:10.1080/1057610X.2012.639062.

Mohamedou, M. 2018. *A Theory of ISIS: Political Violence and the Transformation of the Global Order*. London: Pluto Press.

Molano, A. 2000. "The evolution of the Farc: A guerrilla group's long history". *NACLA Report on the Americas* 34(2): 23–31. doi:10.1080/10714839.2000.11722627.

Morse, J. 2019. "Blacklists, market enforcement, and the global regime to combat terrorist financing". *International Organization* 73(3): 511–45. doi:10.1017/S002081831900016X.

Mullan, P. 2014. *The Digital Currency Challenge: Shaping Online Payment Systems through US Financial Regulations*. London: Palgrave Macmillan Pivot.

Naghavi, N. 2020. *State of the Industry Report on Mobile Money 2019*. London: GSM Association.

Nance, M. 2015. "Naming and shaming in financial regulation: explaining variation in the Financial Action Task Force on money laundering". In H. Friman (ed.), *The Politics of Leverage in International Relations: Name, Shame, and Sanction*, 123–42. London: Palgrave Macmillan.

Nance, M. 2018. "The regime that FATF built: an introduction to the Financial Action Task Force". *Crime, Law and Social Change* 69(2): 109–29. doi:10.1007/s10611-017-9747-6.

Napoleoni, L. 2007. "Terrorism financing in Europe". In J. Giraldo & H. Trinkunas (eds), *Terrorism Financing and State Responses: A Comparative Perspective*, 171–84. Stanford, CA: Stanford University Press.

National Commission on Terrorist Attacks upon the United States 2004. *The 9/11 Commission Report*. Washington, DC: National Commission on Terrorist Attacks upon the United States.

Nesser, P. 2015. *Islamist Terrorism in Europe: A History*. London: Hurst.

Neumann, P. 2017a. "Don't follow the money: the problem with the war on terrorist financing". *Foreign Affairs* 63(4): 93–102.

Neumann, P. 2017b. "Neumann replies". *Foreign Affairs* 96(6): 149–50.

Norman, S. 2018. "Narcotization as security dilemma: the FARC and drug trade in Colombia". *Studies in Conflict & Terrorism* 41(8): 638–59. doi:10.1080/1057610X.2017.1338052.

Nougayrede, D. 2019. "Anti-money laundering and lawyer regulation: the response of the professions". *Fordham International Law Journal* 43(2): 321–62.

Office of Public Affairs 2020. "Global disruption of three terror finance cyber-enabled campaigns". Washington, DC: US Department of Justice.

Omelicheva, M. & L. Markowitz 2021. "Rethinking intersections of crime and terrorism: insights from political economies of violence". *International Studies Review* 23(4): 1541–65. doi:10.1093/isr/viab025.

Orozco, M., L. Porras & J. Yansura 2019. "Remittances to Latin America and the Caribbean in 2018". Washington, DC: Inter-American Dialogue. https://www.thedialogue.org/analysis/remittances-to-latin-america-and-the-caribbean-in-2018/ (accessed 17 April 2019).

Oxnevad, I. 2016. "The caliphate's gold: the Islamic State's monetary policy and its implications". *Journal of the Middle East and Africa* 7(2): 125–40. doi:10.1080/21520844.2016.1191051.

Pokalova, E. 2019. "Driving factors behind foreign fighters in Syria and Iraq". *Studies in Conflict & Terrorism* 42(9): 798–818. doi:10.1080/1057610X.2018.1427842.

Pol, R. 2020. "Anti-money laundering: the world's least effective policy experiment? Together, we can fix it". *Policy Design and Practice* 3(1): 73–94. doi:10.1080/25741292.2020.1725366.

Powell, C. 2018. "The United Nations Security Council sanctions regime against the financing of terrorism". In C. King, C. Walker & J. Gurulé (eds), *The Palgrave Handbook of Criminal and Terrorism Financing Law*, 883–906. London: Palgrave Macmillan.

Pozsar, Z. *et al.* 2013. "Shadow banking". *FRBNY Economic Policy Review* 19(2): 1–16. https://www.newyorkfed.org/research/epr/2013/0713adri.html (accessed 24 June 2021).

Pragg-Jaggernauth, R. *et al.* 2019. "De-risking in the Caribbean region: a CFATF perspective". Port of Spain, Trinidad and Tobago: Caribbean Financial Action Task Force.

Prost, K. 2018. "The intersection of AML/SFT and Security Council sanctions". In C. King, C. Walker & J. Gurulé (eds), *Palgrave Handbook of Criminal and Terrorism Financing Law*, 907–26. London: Palgrave Macmillan.

Rabasa, A. & P. Chalk 2001. "Colombian labyrinth: the synergy of drugs and insurgency and its implications for regional stability". Monograph Reports. Santa Monica: Rand Corporation.

Raphaeli, N. 2003. "Financing of terrorism: sources, methods, and channels". *Terrorism and Political Violence* 15(4): 59–82.

Ratha, D. *et al.* 2021. "Resilience: COVID-19 crisis through a migration lens". Migration and Development Brief. Washington, DC: KNOMAD-World Bank.

RDWTI 2009. "RAND Database of Worldwide Terrorism Incidents". Santa Monica: RAND Corporation.

Reuter, P. & E. Truman 2004. *Chasing Dirty Money: The Fight Against Money Laundering*. Washington, DC: Institute for International Economics.

Robinson, P. 2004. "Anti-money laundering regulation: next generation developments". Text of speech to the City & Financial Conference. https://webarchive.nationalarchives.gov.uk/ 20081231150201/http://www.fsa.gov.uk/Pages/Library/Communication/Speeches/2004/ sp180.shtml (accessed 16 June 2021).

Rogoff, K. 2016. *The Curse of Cash*. Princeton, NJ: Princeton University Press.

Romaniuk, P. & T. Keatinge 2018. "Protecting charities from terrorists ... and counterterrorists: FATF and the global effort to prevent terrorist financing through the non-profit sector". *Crime, Law and Social Change* 69(2): 265–82. doi:10.1007/ s10611-017-9755-6.

Rosand, E. 2005. "The Security Council as "global legislator": ultra vires or ultra innovative?" *Fordham International Law Journal* 28: 542–90.

Ross, M. 1991. "Bankers, guns, and money: financial assistance for terrorism under the prevention of Terrorism Act, 1989". *Boston College International and Comparative Law Review* 14(1): 77–110.

Roth, J., D. Greenburg & S. Wille 2004. *Monograph on Terrorist Financing*. Washington, DC: National Commission on Terrorist Attacks on the United States.

Russo, A. & S. Giusti 2019. "The securitisation of cultural heritage". *International Journal of Cultural Policy* 25(7): 843–57. doi:10.1080/10286632.2018.1518979.

Ryder, N. 2015. *The Financial War on Terrorism: A Review of Counter-Terrorist Financing Strategies since 2001*. Abingdon: Routledge.

Sands, P. 2016. "Making it harder for the bad guys: the case for eliminating high denomination notes". M-RCBG Associate Working Paper series, Mossavar-Rahmani Center for Business & Government, Harvard Kennedy School.

Sanín, F. 2006. "Internal conflict, terrorism and crime in Colombia". *Journal of International Development* 18(1): 137–50. doi:10.1002/jid.1267.

Schindler, H. 2020. "United Nations and counter-terrorism: strategy, structure and prevention of violent extremism conducive to terrorism: a practitioner's view". In S. Hansen & S. Lid (eds), *Routledge Handbook of Deradicalisation and Disengagement*, 163–79. Abingdon: Routledge.

Sciolino, E. 2008. "In '06 bomb plot trial, a question of imminence". *The New York Times*, 15 July. https://www.nytimes.com/2008/07/15/world/europe/15terror.html (accessed 14 December 2021).

Scott, S. & M. Zachariadis 2012. "Origins and development of SWIFT, 1973–2009". *Business History* 54(3): 462–82. doi:10.1080/00076791.2011.638502.

Shabi, R. 2015. "Looted in Syria – and sold in London: the British antiques shops dealing in artefacts smuggled by Isis". *The Guardian*, 3 July. https://www.theguardian.com/world/2015/ jul/03/antiquities-looted-by-isis-end-up-in-london-shops (accessed 14 February 2017).

Sharman, J. 2009. "The bark is the bite: international organisations and blacklisting". *Review of International Political Economy* 16(4): 573–96.

Sharman, J. 2011. *The Money Laundry: Regulating Criminal Finance in the Global Economy*. Ithaca, NY: Cornell University Press.

Shatz, H. & E. Johnson 2015. *The Islamic State We Knew: Insights Before the Resurgence and their Implications*. Santa Monica, CA: RAND Corporation.

Shaw, J. 2000. *Law of the European Union*. Third edn. Basingstoke: Palgrave Macmillan.

Simpson, G. 2006. "Treasury tracks financial data in secret program". *The Wall Street Journal*, 23 June. https://www.wsj.com/articles/SB115101988281688182 (accessed 15 July 2021).

Singh, R. 2017. "A preliminary typology mapping pathways of learning and innovation by modern jihadist groups". *Studies in Conflict & Terrorism* 40(7): 624–44. doi:10.1080/1057610X.2016.1237228.

Smyth, J. 2013. "Security: smoking out the smugglers". *Financial Times*, 1 September.

Solomon, E. 2015a. "The Isis economy: meet the new boss". *Financial Times*, 5 January.

Solomon, E. 2015b. "Upsurge in air strikes threatens Isis oil production". *Financial Times*, 18 November.

Solomon, E. & A. Mhidi 2017a. "The black market trade in Isis fighters". *Financial Times*, 8 January.

Solomon, E. & A. Mhidi 2017b. "Isis finds escape route for the spoils of war". *Financial Times*, 23 August.

Solomon, E. & S. Jones 2015. "Isis Inc: loot and taxes keep jihadi economy churning". *Financial Times*, 14 December.

Solomon, E., G. Chazan & S. Jones 2014. "Isis Inc: how oil fuels the jihadi terrorists". *Financial Times*, 14 October.

Solomon, E., R. Kwong & S. Bernard 2016. "Inside Isis Inc: the journey of a barrel of oil". *Financial Times*, 29 February.

Solomon, J. 2014. "US, allies step up efforts to choke off Islamic State's funding". *The Wall Street Journal*, 9 September. http://online.wsj.com/articles/u-s-allies-step-up-efforts-to-choke-off-islamic-states-funding-1410307008 (accessed 13 September 2014).

Staibano, C. 2005. "Trends in UN Sanctions: from ad hoc practice to institutional capacity building". In P. Wallensteen & C. Staibano (eds), *International Sanctions: Between Words and Wars in the Global System*, 31–54. London: Frank Cass.

Stothard, M. 2015. "France seeks new powers to monitor terror suspects' bank accounts". *Financial Times*, 23 November.

Sun, M. 2020. "Banks navigate hazy regulations to serve cannabis businesses". *The Wall Street Journal*, 26 October. https://www.wsj.com/articles/banks-navigate-hazy-regulations-to-serve-cannabis-businesses-11603704601 (accessed 20 February 2021).

Symington, J., M. Thom & A. van der Linden 2020. "Inclusive AML-CFT Models in Africa: lessons from six financial service providers". Cenfri.

Talley, I. & B. Faucon 2020. "Islamic State, defeated US foe, still brims with cash, ambition". *The Wall Street Journal*, 18 September. https://www.wsj.com/articles/islamic-state-defeated-u-s-foe-still-brims-with-cash-ambition-11600464409 (accessed 20 September 2020).

Taylor, J. 2007. *Global Financial Warriors: The Untold Story of International Finance in the Post-9/11 World*. New York, NY: Norton.

Theodorou, Y. 2013. "The mandatory registration of prepaid SIM card users". London: GSM Association.

Thoumi, F. & M. Anzola 2010. "Asset and money laundering in Bolivia, Columbia and Peru: a legal transplant in vulnerable environments?" *Crime, Law and Social Change* 53(5): 437–55.

Tilly, C. 1985. "War making and state making as organized crime". In D. Rueschemeyer, P. Evans & T. Skocpol (eds), *Bringing the State Back In*, 169–91. Cambridge: Cambridge University Press.

Tokar, D. 2021. "US solicits public feedback on anti-money-laundering rules for antiquities dealers". *The Wall Street Journal*, 23 September. https://www.wsj.com/articles/u-s-solicits-public-feedback-on-anti-money-laundering-rules-for-antiquities-dealers-11632422996 (accessed 3 October 2021).

Truell, P. 1996. "In case tied to Mexico, witness from Citibank is called a liar". *The New York Times*, 4 December. https://www.nytimes.com/1996/12/04/world/in-case-tied-to-mexico-witness-from-citibank-is-called-a-liar.html (accessed 15 June 2022).

Tsingou, E. 2015. "Club governance and the making of global financial rules". *Review of International Political Economy* 22(2): 225–56. doi:10.1080/09692290.2014.890952.

Tsingou, E. 2018. "New governors on the block: the rise of anti-money laundering professionals". *Crime, Law and Social Change* 69(2): 191–205. doi:10.1007/s10611-017-9751-x.

Turner, J. 2009. "Blocking faith, freezing charity: chilling Muslim charitable giving in the 'war on terrorism financing'". New York, NY: American Civil Liberties Union.

US Treasury 2021. "Treasury designates al-Qa'ida support network in Brazil". Washington, DC, last revised 22 December. https://home.treasury.gov/news/press-releases/jy0546 (accessed 27 December 2021).

United Nations General Assembly 2006. "Uniting against terrorism: recommendations for a global counter-terrorism strategy". In A/60/825. New York, NY. https://undocs.org/A/60/825 (accessed 10 August 2021).

United Nations Secretary-General 2001. "Press encounter following adoption of Security Council Resolution 1368 condemning terrorist attacks in the USA". New York, NY. https://www.un.org/sg/en/content/sg/press-encounter/2001-09-12/press-encounter-following-adoption-security-council-resolution (accessed 10 August 2021).

United Nations Secretary-General 2020. "Eleventh report of the Secretary-General on the threat posed by ISIL (Da'esh) to international peace and security and the range of United Nations efforts in support of Member States in countering the threat". New York, NY. https://digitallibrary.un.org/record/3874983?ln=en (accessed 12 November 2021).

United States Fire Administration 1993. *The World Trade Center Bombing: Report and Analysis.* Washington, DC: Federal Emergency Management Agency.

Uniting and Strengthening America by Providing Appropriate Tools Required to Intercept and Obstruct Terrorism (USA PATRIOT) Act of 2001. U.S. Public Law 107-56. 115, 26 October 2001.

van Duyne, P., J. Harvey & L. Gelemerova 2018. *The Critical Handbook of Money Laundering: Policy, Analysis and Myths.* London: Palgrave Macmillan.

Viswanatha, A. & G. Kantchev 2017. "US files suit to seize antiquities looted by Islamic State militants". *The Wall Street Journal*, 6 December. https://www.wsj.com/articles/u-s-tries-to-seize-antiquities-looted-by-islamic-state-and-used-to-fund-terrorism-1512584097 (accessed 15 January 2018).

Vittori, J. 2011. *Terrorist Financing and Resourcing.* Basingstoke: Palgrave Macmillan.

Vlcek, W. 2009. "Hitting the right target: EU and Security Council pursuit of terrorist financing". *Critical Studies on Terrorism* 2(2): 275–91.

Waldron, J. 2003. "Security and liberty: the image of balance". *Journal of Political Philosophy* 11(2): 191–210.

Wallensteen, P. & C. Staibano (eds) 2005. *International Sanctions: Between Words and Wars in the Global System.* London: Frank Cass.

Wallensteen, P. & G. Helena 2012. "Targeting the right targets? The UN use of individual sanctions". *Global Governance* 18(2): 207–30. doi:10.1163/19426720-01802005.

Warde, I. 2007. *The Price of Fear: Al-Qaeda and the Truth Behind the Financial War on Terror.* London: I. B. Tauris.

Waters, R. & H. Murphy 2019. "Facebook's full-frontal assault on finance". *Financial Times*, 24 June.

Wechsler, W. 2001. "Follow the money". *Foreign Affairs* 80(4): 40–57.

Weiser, B. 1998. "Saudi is indicted in bomb attacks on US embassies". *The New York Times*, 5 November. https://www.nytimes.com/1998/11/05/world/saudi-is-indicted-in-bomb-atta cks-on-us-embassies.html (accessed 11 June 2021).

Whitlock, C. 2008. "Terrorism financing blacklists at risk". *The Washington Post*, 2 November. https://www.washingtonpost.com/wp-dyn/content/article/2008/11/01/AR2008110102 214.html (accessed 19 March 2009).

Wilder, H. 2019. "Cracking the code: tracing the Bitcoins from a Hamas terrorist fundraising campaign". Elliptic Blog, 26 April. https://www.elliptic.co/blog/tracing-bitcoin-terrorism (accessed 10 February 2021).

Wilkinson, P. 1984. "State-sponsored international terrorism: the problems of response". *The World Today* 40(7): 292–8.

Wilkinson, P. 2009. "The transnational terrorism threat to Europe: an interim assessment". In F. Eder & M. Senn (eds), *Europe and Transnational Terrorism: Assessing Threats and Countermeasures*, 21–34. Baden-Baden: Nomos.

Williams, P. 2008. "Terrorist financing and organized crime: nexus, appropriation, or transformation?" In T. Biersteker & S. Eckert (eds), *Countering the Financing of Terrorism*, 126–49. London: Routledge.

Woodford, I. & M. Smith 2018. "The political economy of the Provos: inside the finances of the Provisional IRA – a revision". *Studies in Conflict & Terrorism* 41(3): 213–40. doi:10.1080/1057610X.2017.1283195.

Working Group on Risk, Compliance and Financial Inclusion 2017. "Report of the survey to assess the existence, causes and impact of de-risking within the Eastern and Southern Africa Anti-Money Laundering Group (ESAAMLG) region". Dar es Salaam, Tanzania: Eastern and Southern Africa Anti-Money Laundering Group.

World Bank 2003. *Global Development Finance: Striving for Stability in Development Finance*. Vol. 1. Washington, DC: IBRD/World Bank.

World Bank 2021. "Defying predictions, remittance flows remain strong during COVID-19 crisis". Washington, DC: World Bank Group.

Wright, A. 2016. *De-Risking and its Impact: The Caribbean Perspective*. St Augustine, Trinidad and Tobago: Caribbean Centre for Money and Finance.

Yikona, S. *et al.* 2011. *Ill-Gotten Money and the Economy: Experiences from Malawi and Namibia*. Washington, DC: World Bank.

Yuniar, R. 2017. "Bitcoin, PayPal used to finance terrorism, Indonesian agency says". *The Wall Street Journal*, 10 January. https://www.wsj.com/articles/bitcoin-paypal-used-to-finance-terrorism-indonesian-agency-says-1483964198 (accessed 3 February 2017).

Zagaris, B. 2002. "Somali Swedes challenge terrorism freeze procedures". *International Enforcement Law Reporter* 18(7): 277–9.

Zelizer, V. 1989. "The social meaning of money: 'special monies'". *American Journal of Sociology* 95(2): 342–77.

Zetter, K. 2009. "Bullion and bandits: the improbable rise and fall of E-Gold". Wired, 9 June. https://www.wired.com/2009/06/e-gold/ (accessed 1 October 2021).

INDEX